-----------------------

was received into the Novitiate of the
Secular Franciscan Order.

_____19_____

-------------------------------------------------------

and admitted to holy Profession

_____19_____

-------------------------------------------------------

# ✝ Secular ✝ Franciscan Companion

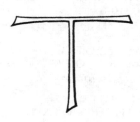

**FRANCISCAN HERALD PRESS**
*Publishers of Franciscan Literature*
**CHICAGO, ILLINOIS**

SECULAR FRANCISCAN COMPANION, compiled and edited by Marion A. Habig, O.F.M., revised. Copyright ©1987 by Franciscan Herald Press, 1434 West 51st Street, Chicago, Illinois 60609. All rights reserved.

**Library of Congress Cataloging-in-Publication Data**
Secular Franciscan companion.
    Rev. ed. of: Tertiary's companion. Rev. ed. 1976, c1961.
    1. Secular Franciscans—Prayer-books and devotions—English.  I. Habig, Marion Alphone, 1901-
    .  II. Tertiary's companion.
BX2050.F7S38  1987      242'.894      87-7495
ISBN 0-8199-0910-6

**Nihil Obstat**
    Mark Hegener, O.F.M.
    Geron Fournelle, O.F.M.
        *Censores Librorum*

**Imprimi Potest**
    Dominic Limacher, O.F.M.
        *Minister Provincial*

**Imprimatur**
    Albert Gregory Meyer, D.D.
        † *Archbishop of Chicago*

**August 11, 1961**

**Revised Edition 1987**
*MADE IN THE UNITED STATES OF AMERICA*

# PREFACE

In the republishing of the SECULAR FRAN-CISCAN COMPANION we have attempted to retain as many as possible of the time-tested prayers that have been so near and dear to the hearts of the Secular Franciscans over the years and which Father Marion Habig, O.F.M., labored so diligently to bring together previously. At the same time we have tried to incorporate the new liturgical directives.

We owe a debt of gratitude both to Father Benet Fonck, O.F.M., for his *Never Cease Praying* as well as to Father Thomas Gardner, O.F.M., for his short history of the Secular Franciscan Order and the model wake service.

It is the hope and the prayer of the publishers

that this recently issued SECULAR FRANCIS-CAN COMPANION will serve as faithfully as did its predecessors.

# CONTENTS

# CALENDAR OF FRANCISCAN SAINTS

# INTRODUCTION

# A SHORT HISTORY OF THE
# SECULAR FRANCISCAN ORDER

St. Francis of Assisi (1182-1226) founded three Orders: The Order of Friars Minor, which is now divided into three branches (Franciscans, Conventuals, Capuchins), with the assistance of St. Clare of Assisi the Order of Poor Ladies or Poor Clares, and—for people living in the world—the Order of Brothers and Sisters in Penance (the Third Order Secular, now known as the Secular Franciscan Order). Out of the last grew the Third Order Regular, comprising numerous congregations of Brothers, and Sisters, as well as a fourth Religious Order of friars (priests and Brothers).

The first simple rule of the Secular Order written by St. Francis was put into legal language by Cardinal Ugolino in 1221, and orally approved the same year by Pope Honorius III. In 1289, Pope Nicholas IV revised the rule and solemnly confirmed it by a papal bull. Pope Leo XIII adapted this rule to the conditions of his time in 1883. In 1978, Pope Paul VI approved a new rule for the Secular Franciscan Order which reflects the task of the universal Church in the modern world and brings the spirit of St. Francis to bear in a creative way on the world today. This rule invites the Secular Franciscan to become a leaven of the gospel in today's world and to take part in its transformation into the kingdom which the Lord Jesus proclaimed.

The Order is comprised of fraternities on various levels made up of men and women, age 21 and older, who have recognized their vocation to the Franciscan Family and strive to achieve holiness in their lay state while bringing the gospel message to the world through the example of their lives. The Secular Franciscan Order has been recommended to the laity by the Supreme Pontiffs of the past century from Pius IX to Paul VI, both by word and example. The Secular Franciscan Order has members in every part of the world; their total number is more than one million.

# SECULAR FRANCISCAN RULE

**Excerpts from:**

## The Rule of the Secular Franciscan Order As Approved and Confirmed by Pope Paul VI

In perpetual remembrance.—The Seraphic Patriarch Saint Francis of Assisi, during his life and even after his beautiful death, not only attracted many to serve God in the religious family founded by him but also drew numerous members of the laity to enter his communities as far as possible while remaining in the world. Moreover, to use the words of our predecessor Pius IX, "it seems . . . that there was never anyone in whom there shone forth more vividly and who resembled more the image of Jesus Christ and the evangelical form of life than Francis" (Encycl. "Rite Expiatis," April 30, 1926; AAS. 18, 1926, p. 154).

We are happy that the "Franciscan Charism"

today is still a force for the good of the Church and the human community, despite the infiltration of doctrines and tendencies that alienate people from God and from the supernatural.

Having consulted with the Sacred Congregation for Religious and Secular Institutes, which has diligently examined and carefully evaluated the text, we approve and confirm with our apostolic authority and sanction the Rule of the Secular Franciscan Order.

By this letter and our apostolic authority, we abrogate the previous rule of what was formerly called the Franciscan Third Order.

Given at Rome at St. Peter's, under the ring of the Fisherman, on June 24, 1978, the 16th year of our pontificate.

JOHN CARDINAL VILLOT
*Secretary of State*

# RULE OF THE
# SECULAR FRANCISCAN ORDER

## PROLOGUE
Exhortation of Saint Francis to the
Brothers and Sisters in Penance.
*In the name of the Lord !*

## CHAPTER I
## CONCERNING THOSE WHO
## DO PENANCE

All who love the Lord with their whole heart,
with their whole soul and mind, with all their
strength (cf. Mk 12:30), and love their neighbors as themselves (cf. Mt 22:39) and hate
their bodies with their vices and sins, and receive the Body and Blood of our Lord Jesus
Christ, and produce worthy fruits of penance:

Oh, how happy and blessed are these men
and women when they do these things and
persevere in doing them, because "the spirit
of the Lord will rest upon them" (cf. Is 11:2)
and he will make "his home and dwelling
among them" (cf. Jn 14:23), and they are the

sons of the heavenly Father (cf. Mt 5:45), whose works they do, and they are the spouses, brothers, and mothers of our Lord Jesus Christ (cf. Mt 12:50).

We are spouses, when by the Holy Spirit the faithful soul is united with our Lord Jesus Christ, we are brothers to him when we fulfill "the will of the Father who is in heaven" (Mt 12:50).

We are mothers, when we carry him in our heart and body (cf. 1 Cor 6:20) through divine love and a pure and sincere conscience; we give birth to him through a holy life which must give light to others by example (cf. Mt 5:16).

Oh, how glorious it is to have a great and holy Father in heaven! Oh, how glorious it is to have such a beautiful and admirable Spouse, the Holy Paraclete!

Oh, how glorious it is to have such a Brother and such a Son, loved, beloved, humble, peaceful, sweet, lovable, and desirable above all: Our Lord Jesus Christ, who gave up his life for his sheep (cf. Jn 10:15) and prayed to the Father saying:

"O holy Father, protect them with your name (cf. Jn 17:11) whom you gave me out of the world. I entrusted to them the message you entrusted to me and they received it. They have known that in truth I came from you, they have believed that it was you who sent me. For these I pray, not for the world (cf. Jn 17:9). Bless and consecrate them, and I consecrate myself for their sakes. I do not pray for them alone; I pray also for those who will believe in me through their word (cf. Jn 17:20) that they may be holy by being one as we are (cf. Jn 17:11). And I desire, Father, to have them in my company where I am to see this glory of mine in your kingdom" (cf. Jn 17:6-24).

# CHAPTER II
# CONCERNING THOSE WHO
# DO NOT DO PENANCE

But all those men and women who are not doing penance and do not receive the Body and Blood of our Lord Jesus Christ and live in vices and sin and yield to evil concupiscence and to the wicked desires of the flesh, and do not observe what they have promised to the Lord, and are slaves to the world, in their bodies, by carnal desires and the anxieties and cares of this life (cf. Jn 8:41):

These are blind, because they do not see the true light, our Lord Jesus Christ; they do not have spiritual wisdom because they do not have the Son of God who is the true wisdom of the Father. Concerning them, it is said, "Their skill was swallowed up" (Ps 107:27) and "cursed are those who turn away from your commands" (Ps 119:21). They see and acknowledge, they know and do bad things and knowingly destroy their own souls.

See, you who are blind, deceived by your enemies, the world, the flesh, and the devil, for it is pleasant to the body to commit sin and it is bitter to make it serve God because all vices and sins come out and "proceed from the heart of man" as the Lord says in the gospel (cf. Mt 7:21). And you have nothing in this world and in the next, and you thought you would possess the vanities of this world for a long time.

But you have been deceived, for the day and the hour will come to which you give no thought and which you do not know and of which you are ignorant. The body grows infirm, death approaches, and so it dies a bitter death, and no matter where or when or how man dies, in the guilt of sin, without penance or satisfaction, though he can make satisfaction but does not do it.

The devil snatches the soul from his body with such anguish and tribulation that no one can know it except he who endures it, and all the talents and power and "knowledge and wisdom" (2 Chr 1:17) which they thought they had will be taken away from them (cf. Lk 8:18; Mk 4:25), and they leave their goods to relatives and friends who take and divide them and say afterwards, "Cursed be his soul because he could have given us more, he could have acquired more than he did." The worms eat up the body and so they have lost body and soul during this short earthly life and will go into the inferno where they will suffer torture without end.

All those into whose hands this letter shall have come to ask in the charity that is God (cf. 1 Jn 4:17) to accept kindly and with divine love the fragrant words of our Lord Jesus Christ quoted above. And let those who do not know how to read have them read to them.

And may they keep them in their mind and carry them out, in a holy manner to the end, because they are "spirit and life" (Jn 6:64).

And those who will not do this will have to

render "an account on the day of judgment"
(cf. Mt 12:36) before the tribunal of our Lord
Jesus Christ (cf. Rom 14:10).

(Cajetan Esser O.F.M., *Die Opuscula
des hl. Franziskus von Assisi.* Nuova
Ediz. Critica, Grottaferrata, 1976;
translated by Marion A. Habig O.F.M.)

# CHAPTER I
# THE SECULAR FRANCISCAN
# ORDER (S.F.O.)[1]

1. The Franciscan family, as one among
many spiritual families raised up by the Holy
Spirit in the Church,[2] unites all members of the
people of God—laity, religious, and priests—
who recognize that they are called to follow
Christ in the footsteps of Saint Francis of
Assisi.[3]

In various ways and forms but in life-giving
union with each other, they intend to make
present the charism of their common Seraphic
Father in the life and mission of the Church.[4]

2. The Secular Franciscan Order holds a
special place in this family circle. It is an
organic union of all Catholic fraternities

scattered throughout the world and open to every group of the faithful. In these fraternities the brothers and sisters, led by the Spirit, strive for perfect charity in their own secular state. By their profession they pledge themselves to live the gospel in the manner of Saint Francis by means of this rule approved by the Church.[5]

3. The present rule, succeeding "Memoriale Propositi" (1221) and the rules approved by the Supreme Pontiffs Nicholas IV and Leo XIII, adapts the Secular Franciscan Order to the needs and expectations of the Holy Church in the conditions of changing times. Its interpretation belongs to the Holy See and its application will be made by the General Constitutions and particular statutes.

# CHAPTER II
# THE WAY OF LIFE

4. The rule and life of the Secular Franciscans is this: to observe the gospel of our Lord Jesus Christ by following the example of Saint Francis of Assisi, who made Christ the inspiration and the center of his life with God and people.[6]

Christ, the gift of the Father's love, is the way to him, the truth into which the Holy Spirit leads us, and the life which he has come to give abundantly.[7]

Secular Franciscans should devote themselves especially to careful reading of the gospel, going from gospel to life and life to the gospel.[8]

5. Secular Franciscans, therefore, should seek to encounter the living and active person of Christ in their brothers and sisters, in Sacred Scripture, in the Church, and in liturgical activity. The faith of Saint Francis, who often said "I see nothing bodily of the Most High Son of God in this world except his most holy body and blood," should be the inspiration and pattern of their Eucharistic life.

6. They have been made living members of the Church by being buried and raised with Christ in baptism; they have been united more intimately with the Church by profession. Therefore, they should go forth as witnesses and instruments of her mission among all people, proclaiming Christ by their life and words.

Called like Saint Francis to rebuild the Church and inspired by his example, let them devote themselves energetically to living in full communion with the pope, bishops, and priests, fostering an open and trusting dialogue of apostolic effectiveness and creativity.[9]

7. United by their vocation as "brothers and sisters of penance,"[10] and motivated by the dynamic power of the gospel, let them conform their thoughts and deeds to those of Christ by means of that radical interior change which the gospel itself calls "conversion." Human frailty makes it necessary that this conversion be carried out daily.[11]

On this road to renewal the sacrament of reconciliation is the privileged sign of the Father's mercy and the source of grace.[12]

8. As Jesus was the true worshipper of the Father, so let prayer and contemplation be the soul of all they are and do.[13]

Let them participate in the sacramental life of the Church, above all the Eucharist. Let them join in liturgical prayer in one of the forms proposed by the Church, reliving the mysteries of the life of Christ.

9. The Virgin Mary, humble servant of the Lord, was open to his every word and call. She was embraced by Francis with indescribable love and declared the protectress and advo-

cate of his family.[14] The Secular Franciscans should express their ardent love for her by imitating her complete self-giving and by praying earnestly and confidently.[15]

10. United themselves to the redemptive obedience of Jesus, who placed his will into the Father's hands, let them faithfully fulfill the duties proper to their various circumstances of life.[16] Let them also follow the poor and crucified Christ, witness to him even in difficulties and persecutions.[17]

11. Trusting in the Father, Christ chose for himself and his mother a poor and humble life,[18] even though he valued created things attentively and lovingly. Let the Secular Franciscans seek a proper spirit of detachment from temporal goods by simplifying their own material needs. Let them be mindful that according to the gospel they are stewards of the goods received for the benefit of God's children.

Thus, in the spirit of "the Beatitudes," and as pilgrims and strangers on their way to the home of the Father,[19] they should strive to purify their hearts from every tendency and yearning for possession and power.

12. Witnessing to the good yet to come and

obliged to acquire purity of heart because of the vocation they have embraced, they should set themselves free to love God and their brothers and sisters.[20]

13. As the Father sees in every person the features of his Son, the firstborn of many brothers and sisters,[21] so the Secular Franciscans with a gentle and courteous spirit accept all people as a gift of the Lord[22] and an image of Christ.

A sense of community will make them joyful and ready to place themselves on an equal basis with all people, especially with the lowly for whom they shall strive to create conditions of life worthy of people redeemed by Christ.[23]

14. Secular Franciscans, together with all people of good will, are called to build a more fraternal and evangelical world so that the kingdom of God may be brought about more effectively. Mindful that anyone "who follows Christ, the perfect man, becomes more of a man himself," let them exercise their responsibilities competently in the Christian spirit of service.[24]

15. Let them individually and collectively be in the forefront in promoting justice by the testimony of their human lives and their

courageous initiatives. Especially in the field of public life, they should make definite choices in harmony with their faith.[25]

16. Let them esteem work both as a gift and as a sharing in the creation, redemption, and service of the human community.[26]

17. In their family they should cultivate the Franciscan spirit of peace, fidelity, and respect for life, striving to make of it a sign of a world already renewed in Christ.[27]

By living the grace of matrimony, husbands and wives in particular should bear witness in the world to the love of Christ for his Church. They should joyfully accompany their children on their human and spiritual journey by providing a simple and open Christian education and being attentive to the vocation of each child.[28]

18. Moreover they should respect all creatures, animate and inanimate, which "bear the imprint of the Most High,"[29] and they should strive to move from the temptation of exploiting creation to the Franciscan concept of universal kinship.

19. Mindful that they are bearers of peace which must be built up unceasingly, they should seek out ways of unity and fraternal

harmony through dialogue, trusting in the presence of the divine seed in everyone and in the transforming power of love and pardon.[30]

Messengers of perfect joy in every circumstance, they should strive to bring joy and hope to others.[31]

Since they are immersed in the resurrection of Christ, which gives true meaning to Sister Death, let them serenely tend toward the ultimate encounter with the Father.[32]

# CHAPTER III
# LIFE IN FRATERNITY

20. The Secular Franciscan Order is divided into fraternities of various levels—local, regional, national, and international. Each one has its own moral personality in the Church.[33] These various fraternities are coordinated and united according to the norm of this rule and of the constitutions.

21. On various levels, each fraternity is animated and guided by a council and minister (or president) who are elected by the professed according to the constitutions.[34]

Their service, which lasts for a definite

period, is marked by a ready and willing spirit and is a duty of responsibility to each member and to the community.

Within themselves the fraternities are structured in different ways according to the norm of the constitutions, according to the various needs of their members and their regions, and under the guidance of their respective council.

22. The local fraternity is to be established canonically. It becomes the basic unit of the whole Order and a visible sign of the Church, the community of love. This should be the privileged place for developing a sense of Church and the Franciscan vocation and for enlivening the apostolic life of its members.[35]

23. Requests for admission to the Secular Franciscan Order must be presented to the local fraternity, whose council decides upon the acceptance of new brothers and sisters.[36]

Admission into the Order is gradually attained through a time of initiation, a period of formation of at least one year, and profession of the rule.[37] The entire community is engaged in this process of growth by its own manner of living. The age for profession and the distinctive Franciscan sign[38] are regulated by the statutes.

Profession by its nature is a permanent commitment.[39]

Members who find themselves in particular difficulties should discuss their problems with the council in fraternal dialogue.

Withdrawal or permanent dismissal from the Order, if necessary, is an act of the fraternity council according to the norm of the constitutions.[40]

24. To foster communion among members, the council should organize regular and frequent meetings of the community as well as meeting with other Franciscan groups, especially with youth groups. It should adopt appropriate means for growth in Franciscan and ecclesial life and encourage everyone to a life of fraternity.[41] This communion continues with deceased brothers and sisters through prayer for them.[42]

25. Regarding expenses necessary for the life of the fraternity and the needs of worship, of the apostolate, and of charity, all the brothers and sisters should offer a contribution according to their means. Local fraternities should contribute toward the expense of the higher fraternity councils.[43]

26. As a concrete sign of communion and

coresponsibility, the councils on various levels, in keeping with the constitutions, shall ask for suitable and well prepared religious for spiritual assistance. They should make this request to the superiors of the four religious Franciscan families, to whom the Secular Fraternity has been united for centuries.

To promote fidelity to the charism as well as observance of the rule and to receive greater support in the life of the fraternity, the minister or president, with the consent of the council, should take care to ask for a regular pastoral visit by the competent religious superiors[44] as well as for a fraternal visit from those of the higher fraternities, according to the norm of the constitutions.

> *"May whoever observes all this be filled in heaven with the blessing of the most high Father, and on earth with that of his beloved Son, together with the Holy Spirit, the Comforter."*
> (Blessing of St. Francis from the Testament)

# NOTES FOR THE NEW RULE

1.  Known also by the name "The Secular Franciscan Fraternity" or by the abbreviation "T.O.F." which corresponds to Third Order Franciscan.
2.  Vatican II, *Lumen Gentium* (Dogmatic Constitution on the Church), 43 (abbr: Church).
3.  Pius XII, Allocution to Tertiaries ("*Nel darvi*"), #1 (July 1, 1956); *Acta Apostolicae Sedis* (abbr: AAS), vol. 48, pp. 574-575.
4.  Vatican II, *Apostolicam Actuositatem* (Decree on the Apostolate of the Laity), 4m (abbr: Laity).
5.  Code of Canon Law, 702:1.
6.  1 Cel 18 (*Omnibus*, p. 244), 115 (*Omnibus*, p. 329) (Abbr: O.).
7.  Jn 3:16, 14:6.
8.  Laity, 30h.
9.  Paul VI, Allocution to Tertiaries ("*Salutiamo volentieri*"), #3 (May 19, 1971); AAS, vol. 63, pp. 545-546.
10. Primitive Rule of the Third Order of St. Francis (abbr: Prim. Rule).
11. Church, 8.
12. Vatican II, *Presbyterorum Ordinis* (Decree on the Ministry and Life of Priests), 18b.
13. Laity, 4a, b, c.
14. 2 Cel 198 (O., p. 521).
15. Church, 67; Laity, 40.
16. Church, 41.
17. Church, 42b.
18. St. Francis, "Letter to All the Faithful," 5 (O., p. 93).
19. Rom 8:17; Church, 48.

20. St. Francis, "Admonitions," 16, (O., p. 83-84); "Letter to All the Faithful," 70 (O., p. 98).
21. Rom 8:29.
22. 2 Cel 85 (O., p. 433); "Letter to All the Faithful," 26 (O., p. 94); 1 OFM Rule, 7: 13 (O., p. 38).
23. 1 OFM Rule, 9:3 (O., 39); Mt 25:40.
24. Church, 31; Vatican II, *Gaudium et Spes* (Pastoral Constitution on the Church in the Modern World), 93 (abbr: Church Today).
25. Laity, 14.
26. Church Today, 67:2; 1 OFM Rule, 7:4 (O., p. 37); 2 OFM Rule, 5:1 (O., p. 61).
27. Rule of Leo XIII, 2:8.
28. Church, 41e; Laity, 30b, c.
29. 1 Cel 80 (O., P. 296).
30. Rule of Leo XIII, 2:9; 3 Comp. 14:58 (O., p. 941).
31. St. Francis, "Admonitions," 21 (O., p. 85); 1 OFM Rule, 7:15 (O., p. 38).
32. Church Today, 78:1-2.
33. Code of Canon Law, 687.
34. Code of Canon Law, 687.
35. Pius XII, Allocution to Tertiaries ("*Nel darvi*"), #3 (July 1, 1956); AAS, vol. 48, p. 577.
36. Code of Canon Law, 694.
37. Prim. Rule, 29-30.
38. 1 Cel 22 (O., p. 247).
39. Prim. Rule, 31.
40. Code of Canon Law, 696.
41. Code of Canon Law, 697.
42. Prim. Rule, 23.
43. Prim. Rule, 20.
44. Rule of Nicholas IV, chap. 16.

# THE
# SECULAR FRANCISCAN
# AT PRAYER

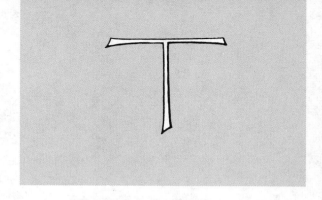

# DAILY PRAYERS

# DAILY PRAYERS

## The Sign of the Cross

In the name of the Father, and of the Son, and of the Holy Spirit. Amen.

## The Our Father

Our Father, who art in heaven; hallowed be thy name; thy kingdom come; thy will be done on earth as it is in heaven; give us this day our daily bread; and forgive us our trespasses, as we forgive those who trespass against us; and lead us not into temptation; but deliver us from evil. Amen.

## The Hail Mary

Hail Mary, full of grace, the Lord is with thee; blessed art thou among women, and blessed is the fruit of thy womb, Jesus. Holy Mary, Mother of God, pray for us sinners, now and at the hour of our death. Amen.

## The Apostles' Creed

I believe in God, the Father almighty, Creator of heaven and earth; and in Jesus Christ, his only Son, our Lord, who was conceived by the Holy Spirit, born of the Virgin Mary; suffered under Pontius Pilate; was crucified, died, and was buried. He descended into hell; the third day he arose again from the dead; he ascended into heaven, sits at the right hand of God, the Father almighty; from thence he shall come to judge the living and the dead. I believe in the Holy Spirit, the holy Catholic Church; the communion of saints, the forgiveness of sins, the resurrection of the body, and life everlasting. Amen.

## The Glory Be

Glory be to the Father, and to the Son, and to the Holy Spirit. As it was in the beginning, is now, and ever shall be, world without end. Amen.

# Acts of Faith, Hope, and Charity

O my God, I firmly believe all the sacred truths which your holy Catholic Church believes and teaches; because you have revealed them, who can neither deceive nor be deceived.

O my God, relying on your infinite goodness and promises, I hope to obtain pardon of my sins, the help of your grace, and life everlasting, through the merits of Jesus Christ, my Lord and Redeemer.

O my God, I love you above all things, with my whole heart, and soul, because you are all good and worthy of love. I love my neighbor as myself for the love of you. I forgive all who have injured me, and ask pardon of all whom I have injured.

## Morning Offering

O Jesus, through the Immaculate Heart of Mary, I offer you my prayers, works, joys, and sufferings of this day for all the intentions of your Sacred Heart, in union with the Holy Sacrifice of the Mass throughout the world, in reparation for my sins, and for the intentions recommended by our Holy Father for this month.

Jesus, meek and humble of heart, make my

heart like unto yours.

O Mary, my Queen, my Mother, I give myself entirely to you, and to show my devotion to you, I consecrate to you this day my eyes, my ears, my mouth, my heart, my whole being, without reserve. Wherefore, good Mother, as I am your own, keep me, guard me as your property and possession. Amen.

St. Joseph, model and patron of those who love the Sacred Heart, pray for me.

## Franciscan Morning Prayer

Jesus Lord, I offer you
this new day because
I believe in you, love you,
hope all things in you
and thank you for
your blessings.
I am sorry for having
offended you and
forgive everyone who
has offended me.
Lord, look on me and
leave in me
peace and courage
and your humble wisdom
that I may serve others
with joy, and be
pleasing to you all day.

## For Parents and Others

O God, who have commanded us to honor father and mother, hear now my humble prayers for my dear parents. Bless them and all their works. Give them the grace to know you, love you, and serve you, that they may be happy with you forever in heaven. Help them teach me what is right, and to give me a good example.

Bless also my brothers and sisters, my schoolmates, my teachers, and all who have been kind to me. Help them all to serve you well, that we all may meet in heaven.

O Jesus, bless also our pastor. Make him a true priest, after your own heart. Give him wisdom to teach me your ways, and reward him for his care of me.

## Grace before Meals

Bless us, O Lord, and these your gifts, which we are about to receive from your goodness. Through Christ our Lord. Amen.

## Grace after Meals

We give thanks, almighty God, for all your benefits, who live and reign world without end. Amen.

# The Rosary

In the name of the Father, etc.

I believe in God, the Father, etc.

Glory be to the Father, etc.

Our Father, etc.

Three Hail Marys, (asking for the grace of faith, hope and charity).

Glory be to the Father, etc.

Then say one Our Father and ten Hail Marys, after which add the Glory be to the Father once for each of the following mysteries:

**I.  The Joyful Mysteries**
>    1. The Annunciation
>    2. The Visitation
>    3. The Nativity
>    4. The Presentation
>    5. The Finding of Jesus in the Temple

**II.  The Sorrowful Mysteries**
>    1. The Agony in the Garden
>    2. The Scourging at the Pillar
>    3. The Crowning with Thorns
>    4. The Carrying of the Cross
>    5. The Crucifixion

**III.  The Glorious Mysteries**
>    1. The Resurrection
>    2. The Ascension
>    3. The Descent of the Holy Spirit
>    5. The Coronation

# FRANCISCAN CROWN ROSARY
## Rosary of the Seven Joys of Mary

Begin the first mystery immediately without any introductory prayers.

1. The angel announces to Mary the birth of the coming Redeemer.
2. The Blessed Virgin Mary visits her cousin Elizabeth.
3. The Savior is born of the Blessed Virgin Mary in the stable of Bethlehem.
4. The Child Jesus is presented in the Temple.
5. The Child Jesus is found in the Temple.
6. The risen Savior appears to the Blessed Virgin on Easter morning.
7. The Blessed Virgin Mary is assumed into heaven and crowned Queen of the Universe.

Add two Hail Marys, in honor of the seventy-two years the Blessed Virgin lived on earth, and one Our Father, Hail Mary, and Glory for the intention of the Holy Father.

## The Angelus

The Angel of the Lord declared unto Mary.
And she conceived by the Holy Spirit.

Hail Mary . . .

Behold the handmaid of the Lord.

Be it done unto me according to your word.

Hail Mary . . .

And the Word was made flesh.

And dwelt among us.

Hail Mary . . .

V. Pray for us, O holy Mother of God.

R. That we may be made worthy of the promises of Christ.

Let us pray:

Pour forth, we beseech you, O Lord, your grace into our hearts, that we, to whom the Incarnation of Christ, your Son, was made known by the message of an angel, may, by his Passion and Cross, be brought to the glory of his Resurrection. Through the same Christ our Lord. Amen.

(*During Eastertime, including Saturday noon before Trinity Sunday, the following is said instead.*)

O Queen of heaven, rejoice, Alleluia.

For he whom you have deserved to bear, Alleluia.

Is risen again, as he said, Alleluia.

Pray for us to God, Alleluia.

V. Rejoice and be glad, O Virgin Mary, Alleluia.

R. Because the Lord is truly risen, Alleluia.

Let us pray:

O God, who, by the resurrection of your Son, our Lord, Jesus Christ, have been pleased to fill the world with joy, grant, we beseech you, that by the Virgin Mary, his Mother, we may receive the joys of eternal life. Through the same Christ our Lord. Amen.

## The Memorare

Remember, O most loving Virgin Mary, that never was it known that anyone who fled to your protection implored your help or sought your intercession, was left unaided. Inspired with this confidence, I fly unto you, O Virgin of Virgins, my Mother! To you I come; before you I stand, sinful and sorrowful. O Mother of the Word Incarnate, despise not my petitions, but in your mercy hear and answer me. Amen.

## Ejaculations

† All for you, Most Sacred Heart of Jesus. Sacred Heart of Jesus, protect our families.
† Jesus, meek and humble of heart, make our hearts like unto yours.
† Heart of Jesus, I place my trust in you.
† Heart of Jesus, burning with love for us, inflame our hearts with love for you.

† Sweet Heart of Jesus, be my love.

† Sweet Heart of Mary, be my salvation.

† O Sacrament most holy
  O Sacrament divine
  All praise and all thanksgiving
  Be every moment thine.

† You are my Mother, O Virgin Mary:
  keep me safe lest I ever offend your dear Son,
  and obtain for me the grace to please him
  always and in all things.

† Jesus, Mary, Joseph, I give you my heart and
  my soul.

† Jesus, Mary, Joseph, assist me in my last
  agony.

† Jesus, Mary, Joseph, may I breathe forth my
  soul in peace with you.

## Necessary Acts

*(This prayer contains all of the "necessary acts," and can be the means of eternal salvation. By helping a dying non-Catholic to pray it sincerely, you can assist him to save his soul.)*

I believe in one God. I believe that God rewards the good and punishes the wicked.

I believe that in God there are three divine persons—God the Father, God the Son, and God the Holy Spirit.

I believe that God the Son became man, without ceasing to be God. I believe that he is my Lord and my Savior, the Redeemer of the human race, that he died on the Cross for the salvation of all.

I believe, on God's authority, everything that he has taught and revealed.

O my God, give me strong faith. O my God, help me to believe with lively faith.

O my God, who are all-good and all-merciful, I sincerely hope to be saved. Help me to do all that is necessary for my salvation.

I have committed many sins in my life, but now I turn away from them and hate them. I am sorry, truly sorry for all of them, because I have offended you, my God, who are all-good, all-perfect, all-holy, all-merciful and kind, and who died on the Cross for me.

I love you, O my God, with all my heart. Please forgive me for having offended you.

I promise, O God, that with your help I will never offend you again.

My God, have mercy on me!

## Night Prayers

In the name of the Father, and of the Son, and of the Holy Spirit. Amen. Blessed be the holy and undivided Trinity now and forever.

## Thanksgiving for the Day

How shall I be able to thank you, O Lord, for all your favors? You have thought of me from all eternity; you have brought me forth from nothing; you have given your life to redeem me, and you continue still, daily, to load me with your favors. My God, what return can I make you for your benefits and in particular for the favors of this day? Join me, you blessed spirits and all the elect, in praising the God of mercies who is so bountiful to so unworthy a creature.

## Invocation of the Holy Spirit

O Holy Spirit, eternal source of light, give me light to know the sins I have committed this day and grant me the grace to be truly sorry for them.

*(Here examine your conscience.)*

## Act of Contrition

O my God, I am heartily sorry for all my sins, and I detest them above all things from the bottom of my heart because they displease you, my God, who are most deserving of all my love, for your most amiable and adorable perfections; and I firmly purpose, by your holy grace, nevermore to offend you, and to do all that I can to atone for my sins.

## Petition

Pour down your blessing, O Lord, on your holy Church; on our holy Father, the Pope; on this diocese, our most reverend bishop, and all pastors of souls; on this country; on our rulers and all superiors, temporal and spiritual; on our parents, relatives, benefactors, friends, and enemies. Help the poor, the sick, and the dying; convert the heretics and enlighten the infidels.

O God, Creator and Redeemer of all the faithful, grant to the souls of your servants departed the remission of all their sins, that, through pious supplications, they may obtain that pardon which they have always desired, who live and reign world without end. Amen.

**V.** Vouchsafe, O Lord, this night to keep us without sin.

**R.** Have mercy on us, O Lord, have mercy on us.

Let us pray:

Visit, we beseech you, O Lord, this dwelling, and drive from it all the snares of the enemy. Let your holy Angels dwell herein to preserve us in peace, and may your blessing be upon us forever. Through Jesus Christ, our Lord. Amen.

## Prayer to be Said before an Image of Jesus Crucified

Behold me, O good and gentle Jesus, while before your face I humbly kneel, and with burning soul, pray and beseech you to fix deep in my heart lively sentiments of faith, hope, and charity, true contrition for my sins, and a firm purpose of amendment, while I contemplate with great love and tender pity your five wounds, pondering over them within me, calling to mind the words which David, your prophet, said of you, my Jesus: "They have pierced my hands and my feet, they have numbered all my bones." (Ps 21: 17-18)

## Prayer to Christ the King

O Christ Jesus, I acknowledge you to be the King of the universe. All that has been made is created by you. Exercise over me all your sovereign rights. I hereby renew the promises of my baptism, renouncing Satan and all his works and pomps; and I engage myself to lead henceforth a truly Christian life. And in a special manner do I undertake to bring about the triumph of the rights of God and your Church, so far as in me lies. Divine Heart of Jesus, I offer you my poor actions to obtain the acknowledgment by every heart of your sacred kingly power. In such wise may the kingdom of your peace be firmly established throughout all the earth. Amen.

## Prayer for the Dying

O most merciful Jesus, lover of souls, I pray you by the agony of your Most Sacred Heart and by the sorrows of your Immaculate Mother, cleanse in your Blood the sinners of the whole world who now in their agony and who are to die this day. Amen.

**V.** Heart of Jesus, once in agony.
**R.** Have mercy on the dying.

## Prayer of St. Francis, on Entering or Leaving a Church

We adore you, most holy Lord Jesus Christ, here and in all your churches, which are in the whole world, and we bless you, because by your holy Cross you have redeemed the world.

## Prayer of St. Bernardine of Siena

We fly to your patronage, O holy Mother of God; despise not our prayers in our necessities;

but deliver us always from all dangers, O most glorious and Blessed Virgin, our Queen, our Mediatress, our Advocate; reconcile us to your Son, commend us to your Son, present us to your Son.

My Guardian Angel, watch over me this night. St. Joseph, my Patron, St. Francis, and all you angels and saints of God, pray for me.

Into your hands, O Lord, I commend my spirit. Save me waking, and keep me sleeping that I may watch with Christ and rest in peace. Amen.

O my dear Jesus, deign to accept the offering I present to you.

## Act of Petition

O bounteous source of all goodness, what can you refuse me after giving yourself wholly to me? Grant me, O divine Jesus, to persevere in your holy love. Give me still greater sorrow for my past sins, and strengthen the sincere resolution I have formed never again to offend you. Hear the prayers I address to you for your Holy Church, for our Holy Father the Pope, for my dear parents, relatives, friends and enemies, and for the suffering souls in purgatory.

# Soul of Christ

Soul of Christ, sanctify me.
Body of Christ, save me.
Blood of Christ, inebriate me.
Water from the side of Christ, wash me.
Passion of Christ, strengthen me.
O good Jesus, hear me.
Within thy wounds hide me.
Permit me not to be separated from thee.
From the malignant enemy defend me.
In the hour of my death call me.
And bid me come to thee.
That with thy saints I may praise thee forever and ever. Amen.

# Prayers of St. Francis
## Ejaculations

† My God and my all!

† My God and my all! Who are you, O God most dear, and who am I, your worthless, useless, little worm of a servant!

† You are my God. Teach me to do your will!

† Lord, be merciful to me, a sinner!

† Lord, take pity on my infirmities, so that I may be able to bear them patiently!

† You are my Father, most holy, my King and my God!

## Prayers in Trials and Suffering
### 1.

I give you thanks, O Lord God, for these pains of mine, and I beg you, my Lord, add a hundred-fold to them if it please you. It will be most agreeable to me that in afflicting me with pain you do not spare me. Fulfilling your holy will is more than ample comfort to me.

### 2.

O my Lord Jesus Christ, I thank you for the great love you have shown me. For it is a token of great love if the Lord punishes his servant well for his faults in this life, so that he may not be punished in the next.

## Prayers to Fulfill God's Will
### 1.

Almight, eternal, just, and merciful God, grant that we do what we know you want, and that we always want whatever is pleasing to you, so that cleansed interiorly, interiorly enlightened and aglow with the fire of the Holy Spirit, we may be able to follow the footsteps of your Son, our Lord Jesus Christ. Aided by your soul-saving grace may we be able to attain to you, who in perfect trinity and simple unity live and reign and triumph as God almighty, world without end. Amen.

### 2.

O great God of glory, my Lord Jesus Christ, I entreat you, put light into the darkness of my mind. Give me the right faith, firm hope, and perfect charity. Help me learn to know you, O Lord, so well that in all things I may do everything in true keeping with your holy will.

### Prayers for the Love of God

#### 1.

Most holy Lord, I should like to love you. O God, I should like to love you. O Lord God, I have given up to you all my heart and my body; and I yearn passionately to do still more for love of you, if only I knew how.

### 2.

Please, O Lord, let the fiery, honeyed force of your love lap up my spirit from everything there is under heaven, so that I may die for love of love for you, who deigned to die for love of love for me.

### 3.

O Lord Jesus Christ, I entreat you to give me

two graces before I die: first, that in my lifetime I may feel in body and soul as far as possible the pain you endured in the hour of your most bitter suffering: and secondly, that I may feel in my heart as far as possible that excess of love by which you, O Son of God, were inflamed to undertake so cruel a suffering for us sinners.

## Paraphrase of the Our Father

*Our Father,* most holy, our Creator, our Redeemer and Savior, our Comforter.

*Who are in heaven,* in the angels and saints, giving them light to know you, since you, O Lord, are Light; setting them afire to love you, since you, O Lord, are Love; abiding in them and filling them for their bliss, since you, O Lord, are the sovereign Good, the eternal Good, from which everything good has its being and without which there is nothing good.

*Hallowed be your name.* May we grow in our knowledge of you, that we may appreciate the width of your favors and the length of your promises to us as well as the utter height of your majesty and the depth of your judgments.

*Your kingdom come,* so that you may rule in us through grace and have us reach your kingdom, where the sight of you is clear, love of you is perfect, association with you is full of bliss, and enjoyment of you is eternal.

*Your will be done on earth as it is in heaven,* so that we may love you with all our heart by always keeping you in mind; with all our soul by always longing for you; with all our mind by directing all our intentions to you and seeking your glory in everything; and with all our strength by exerting all the forces and faculties of soul and body in your loving service and in nothing else. So may we love our neighbors as ourselves, by getting them all so far as we can to love you, by being as glad at the good fortune of others as at our own, while feeling for their misfortune, and giving no offense to anybody.

*Give us this day our daily bread,* your beloved Son, our Lord Jesus Christ, so that we will remember, understand, and respect the love he bore for us and all he said and did and endured for us.

*And forgive us our trespasses,* in your unutterable mercy, in virtue of the suffering of your beloved Son, our Lord Jesus Christ, and the merits and intercession of the blessed Virgin Mary and all your elect.

*As we forgive those who trespass against us;* and what we do not fully forgive, do you, O Lord, make us forgive fully, so that for your sake we may truly love our enemies and devotedly intercede with you for them, giving nobody evil in return for evil and trying to be helpful toward everybody in your Name.

*And lead us not into temptation,* neither hidden nor apparent, neither sudden nor persistent.

*But deliver us from evil,* past, present, and future.

*Amen.* Glory be to the Father and to the Son and to the Holy Spirit. Amen.

## Praises of God

You alone are holy, O Lord God.

You are he who performs things wondrous.

You are strong.

You are full of majesty.

You are the Most High.

You are the King Almighty—you, holy Father, king of heaven and earth.

You are the Lord God, threefold and one, all that is good.

You are what is good, all that is good, the Sovereign Good, the Lord God, true and living.

You are charity and love.

You are wisdom.

You are humility.

You are patience.

You are assurance.

You are restfulness.

You are joy and gladness.

You are justice and temperance.

You are all the wealth desirable.

You are beauty.

You are gentleness.

You protect.

You guard and defend.

You are fortitude.

You are refreshment.

You are our hope.

You are our faith.

You are our great relish.

You are our eternal life, great and wondrous Lord, God almighty, Savior merciful.

## Praises before the Office

Holy, holy, holy, the Lord God almighty who is and who was and who is to come.

Let us praise and exalt him above all things forever.

You are worthy, O Lord our God, to receive

praise, and glory, and honor, and blessing.

Let us praise and exalt him above all things forever.

Worthy is the Lamb who was slain to receive power and Godhead and wisdom and strength and honor and glory and blessing.

Let us praise and exalt him above all things forever.

Let us bless the Father and the Son with the Holy Spirit.

Let us praise and exalt him above all things forever.

Bless the Lord, all you works of the Lord.

Let us praise and exalt him above all things forever.

Speak your praise to God, all his servants and all you who fear the Lord, little and great.

Let us praise and exalt him above all things forever.

May the heavens and the earth praise him in his glory—and every creature in heaven and on earth and under the earth, together with the sea and everything in it.

Let us praise and exalt him above all things forever.

Glory be to the Father and to the Son and to the Holy Spirit.

Let us praise and exalt him above all things forever.

As it was in the beginning, is now, and ever shall be, world without end. Amen.

Let us praise and exalt him above all things forever.

Almighty, most holy, most high and sovereign God, the sovereign Good, who alone are good, to you let us render all praise, all glory, all thanks, all honor, all blessing, and to you let us refer always whatever is good. Amen.

## Blessing of St. Francis

May the Lord bless us and keep us.

May he show his face to us and have mercy on us.

May he turn his countenance toward us and give us peace.

May the Lord bless us.

## Salutation of the Blessed Virgin Mary

Hail, holy Lady, most holy Queen, Mary, Mother of God, you are forever Virgin, chosen by the most holy Father in heaven, whom he consecrated with his most holy beloved Son and the Paraclete Spirit! You in whom was and is all plenitude of grace and all good! Hail, his palace! Hail, his tabernacle! Hail, his dwelling! Hail, his vesture! Hail, his handmaid! Hail, his Mother—and all you holy Virtues that by the grace and light of the Holy Spirit are infused into the hearts of the faithful, that from faithless souls you may make souls faithful to God!

## Prayers to St. Francis
### For Fidelity to the Rule

Holy father, loving and most beloved St. Francis, I beseech you by the holy wounds of our Lord Jesus Christ, which were imprinted on your body, assist me to govern the five senses of my body according to the will and pleasure of almighty God. Intercede for me, so that I may be most faithful in the observance of your Rule of Penance. Obtain for me contrition and devotion, faith, hope, and charity, patience, and purity of body and soul, together with the grace of persevering in the service of our Lord; so that after this life I may merit to come to you, with you to enjoy eternal happiness, which I hope through your intercession to obtain from Christ our Lord. Amen.

### For the Spirit of Penance

O seraphic father, St. Francis, I venerate in

you the living image of Christ crucified. Your love transformed your whole life into one long martyrdom. It made you strive by means of severe penances to satisfy the ardor of your desires, until at last it impressed on your body the wounds it had long before engraved deeply in your heart. It thus made you a living crucifix, preaching sweetly to all people the sufferings and love of Jesus. Obtain for me, O holy father, that I too may banish from my heart the spirit of the world; that I may esteem poverty and humiliation above wealth and honor; that I may mortify my passions and advance daily in the knowledge and love of God, until at last, detached from myself, from the world and from all creatures, I may live for God alone, and like you say with my whole heart, "My God and my all," my God, my inheritance and my joy in time and eternity. Amen.

## For Detachment

O glorious St. Francis, who even in your youth generously renounced the conveniences and comforts of your home in order to follow Jesus more closely in humility and poverty, in mortification and passionate love of the Cross, and so deserved to see imprinted on your body the miraculous stigmata, obtain for us too, we beg you, the grace here below to pass as if insensible through the fleeting splendor of all worldly things, our heart pulsing steadily with love of Jesus crucified even in the saddest and darkest hours of life and our eye serenely raised to heaven as if already foretasting the possession of the infinite good with its eternal divine joys.

### For Perseverance

O seraphic St. Francis, my beloved father, protector of the poor, glorious founder of your three Orders, with tender love and veneration I kneel before you and kiss the sacred stigmata with which our Divine Savior adorned you. I thank you for having numbered me among your children. It is a grace so sublime that I could never have merited it for myself and it brings with it an endless chain of Heaven's choicest blessings. How shall I ever be able to show you gratitude enough for all these favors?

O holy father, help me always to love the Secular Franciscan Order tenderly. Let me consider it my spiritual home and my paradise on earth, that, ever mindful of my holy profession, I may keep the commandments of God and the

Church, and observe faithfully even the smallest details of the rule. For in that way I shall perceive the wholesome effects of the blessings which you, in your dying hour, invoked on your beloved children. Bless me, therefore, kind father. Bless your unworthy child, that I may persevere in the conscientious observance of the rule of the Secular Franciscan Order till the end of my life. Amen.

## Prayers to Franciscan Saints
### To St. Bonaventure
#### (July 15)

O glorious St. Bonaventure, faithful follower of the holy Patriarch Francis and brightest ornament of his order, by your profound knowledge and ardent love of God, you have merited the title of Seraphic Doctor and added luster to the Franciscan name. By your kindness and humility and gentleness of manner, you have drawn all hearts to you and filled them with a love for virtue.

Teach me, I pray you, to imitate your example and to advance daily in piety and the love of God. Teach me, also, that urbanity of manner and respect for the opinion of others which mark the Christian gentleman, so that I may never, in word or deed, offend my neighbor, but edify him at all times by my good deportment. Amen.

### To St. Paschal Baylon
(May 17)

O blessed Paschal, for your fervent love and tender devotion to your Eucharistic Lord, you have deserved to be chosen by holy Church as patron of all who venerate his Sacred Body and Blood in the adorable Sacrament of the Altar. From your very infancy, you manifested your affection for the Holy Eucharist. As a poor and humble shepherd lad, you were favored with a wonderful apparition of the Sacred Host; and even after death, you were permitted miraculously to adore your Lord and your God in the Sacrifice of holy Mass.

By your own ardent love for this august Sacrament, I beseech you to obtain for me a great love and devotion and reverence for him who has set his tabernacle in our midst, to be our daily food and sacrifice. Through your gracious intercession, I hope to receive the same spiritual fruits that you derived from the frequent reception of this Bread of Life. Pray that It may be, indeed, the Bread of my life, the

Center of all my thoughts, words, desires, actions, and aspirations. Pray that It may be my Viaticum on my last journey through the dark valley of death to the splendors of the heavenly Jerusalem, there to behold face to face him whom now I adore as my hidden God and Savior. Amen.

## To St. Louis
### Patron of the Secular Franciscan Order
(Aug. 25)

O holy King St. Louis, worthy son of our holy father St. Francis and patron of the Secular Franciscan Order, intercede for me with our heavenly Father. Obtain for me the grace to follow in your footsteps, to be always a dutiful child of St. Francis, and to observe exactly, all the days of my life, that holy rule which you loved so ardently and kept so faithfully. Be my guide and protector, so that I may never stray from the path of virtue but increase daily in holiness and perfection, and finally merit to be numbered among the chosen ones of our Seraphic Father in heaven. Amen.

**V.** Pray for us, blessed Louis,

**R.** That we may be made worthy of the promises of Christ.

Let us pray:

O God, who have transferred your confessor blessed Louis from an earthly realm to the glory of the heavenly kingdom, we beseech you that through his merits and intercession we may become the companions of the King of Kings, Jesus Christ, your Son. Who lives and reigns world without end. Amen.

### To St. Elizabeth of Hungary
**Patron of the Secular Franciscan Order**
(Nov. 17)

O dear St. Elizabeth, chosen vessel of sublime virtues. You have shown the world by your splendid example what marvels charity, faith, and humility can perform in a Christian soul.

You spent all the powers of your heart in loving your God alone. You loved him with a love so pure and fervent that it made you worthy here on earth to have a foretaste of those favors and delights of Paradise which are given to the souls invited to the marriage feast of the adorable Lamb of God.

Enlightened by the supernatural light of an unshakable faith, you proved yourself a true child of the gospel; for in your neighbor you beheld the person of our Lord Jesus Christ, the sole object of your love. After his example you found your delight in associating with the poor, waiting on them, drying their tears, comforting their minds, and assisting them with every loving service in the midst of the ailments and other great afflictions to which our human nature is subject.

You made yourself poor to relieve poverty in your neighbor; poor in the goods of this world, to enrich yourself with those of heaven. You were so humble that, after having exchanged a palace for a cell and royal robes for the modest garb of seraphic St. Francis, you did lead, though innocent, a life of privation and penance, embracing cheerfully the Cross of our divine Redeemer, and willingly accepting, as he did, insult and most unjust persecution. You forgot the world and yourself to think only of God.

O most lovable saint, so beloved of God, deign to be the heavenly protector of our soul and help it render itself ever more acceptable to God.

From the heights of heaven cast upon us one of those tender looks which, while you were on earth, so often cured grievous infirmities. In the world in which we live, so indifferent to the things of God, we have recourse to you with confidence: obtain that God may enlighten our minds and strengthen our wills, so that we may secure the peace of our soul.

Protect us in this our perilous pilgrimage. Obtain for us the pardon of our failings, and open for us the way to enter with you and share the kingdom of God. Amen.

# MEDITATIONS

## Before Holy Mass

O Almighty Lord of heaven and earth, behold I presume to appear before you this day, to offer up to you by the hands of this your servant, and by those of our High Priest, Jesus Christ, your Son, the sacrifice of his body and blood; in union with that sacrifice which he offered you on the cross; to your honor, praise, adoration, and glory; in remembrance of his death and passion; in thanksgiving for all your blessings, especially for all those bestowed upon me; to obtain the pardon and remission of all my sins, and of those of the living and the dead, for whom I ought to pray; and lastly, for obtaining all graces and blessings for myself, and for your whole Church. O be pleased to bestow upon me your grace, that I may so commemorate the passion and death of your Son, as to partake most plentifully of its fruits. Through the same Jesus Christ, your Son. Amen.

## Adoration and Praise

"O my God, I adore you; I acknowledge you to be the Lord and Master of my life. I own that whatever I am and possess proceeds from you. Your supreme Majesty deserves infinite honor and homage. I, however, offer you the humiliations and the homage which Jesus presents to you on this altar. What Jesus does, I also intend to do; I humbly prostrate myself with him before your divine Majesty, and praise you as the source of all good that can be found in heaven and on earth. I rejoice, because Jesus renders to you, for me, infinite honor and homage."

## Atonement

"Behold, O my God, the traitor, who so often rebelled against you. With a contrite heart, I abhor and detest my numerous offenses. In atonement for them I offer to you all the merits of Jesus, the Blood of Jesus, yes, Jesus entire—

true God and true man—as he is here sacrificed anew for me. And since Jesus himself becomes, on this altar, my mediator and advocate, I unite my voice with that of his blood, which craves pardon for me, and implore mercy for my numerous and grievous offenses. The Blood of Jesus supplicates for mercy; my contrite heart implores the same. Should my tears not move you, let at least the supplications of Jesus move you to mercy. On the cross, he obtained mercy for the entire human race; on this altar, he will obtain it for me. I sincerely hope that for the sake of that precious blood you will pardon my grievous sins, and in return I will love you for all eternity."

## Thanksgiving

"O most amiable God, I am completely overwhelmed with the benefits, both general and particular, which you have bestowed on me, and which you will continue to bestow in time and in eternity. I acknowledge that your mercy toward me was and is infinite; nevertheless, I desire fully to repay you. Therefore, as a tribute of my gratitude and in discharge of my indebtedness, I offer you, by the hands of the priest, this divine Blood, this divine Body of your Son, as a most guiltless victim. This oblation is all-sufficient to repay you for all the graces you have conferred on me; this gift of infinite value is an equivalent for all the favors I have ever received, or shall yet receive from you. O holy angels and blessed spirits, assist me to thank my God; and in thanksgiving for his many benefits, offer to him not only this Mass, but all the Masses at this moment celebrated throughout the world, that his loving goodness may be fully recompensed for all the graces he has bestowed, and will yet bestow on me, now and for all eternity. Amen."

## Petition

"Most gracious God, I acknowledge that I am utterly unworthy of your favors; I confess that, for my numerous and grievous offenses, I am not worthy to be heard; but it is impossible that you should not listen to your divine Son, who on this altar intercedes for me, and offers for me his life, his blood. My most loving God, hear the prayers of this my advocate, and for his sake grant me all the graces that you know to be necessary for me in the great work of my salvation. I am now encouraged to ask of you a general pardon of all my sins and the grace of final perseverance. Trusting in the merits of my Jesus, I ask of you, O God, all virtues in a heroic degree and all efficacious helps necessary to make me a saint. I ask of you the conversion of all sinners, especially of those related to me. I implore you to grant me and mine the spirit of prayer, that you may henceforth dwell in our hearts as in a paradise, leading us from virtue to virtue on to perfection."

# The Creed
# of Pope Paul VI

WE BELIEVE in one only God, Father, Son and Holy Spirit, Creator of things visible such as this world in which our transient life passes, of things invisible such as the pure spirits which are also called angels, and Creator in each man of his spiritual and immortal soul.

We believe that this only God is absolutely one in his infinitely holy essence as also in all his perfections, in his omnipotence, his infinite knowledge, his providence, his will and his love. He is "He Who Is," as he revealed to Moses; and he is "Love," as the Apostle John teaches us: so that these two names, Being and Love, express ineffably the same divine reality of him who has wished to make himself known to us, and who "dwelling in light inaccessible," is in himself above every name, above every thing and above every created intellect.

GOD ALONE can give us right and full knowledge of this reality by revealing himself as Father, Son and Holy Spirit, in whose eternal life we are by grace called to share, here below in the obscurity of faith and after death in eternal light. The mutual bonds which eternally constitute the three persons, who are each one and the same divine being, are the blessed inmost life of God thrice holy, infinitely beyond all that we can conceive in human measure. We give thanks, however, to the divine goodness that very many believers can testify with us before men to the unity of God, even though they know not the mystery of the Most Holy Trinity.

We believe then in the Father who eternally begets the Son, in the Son, the Word of God, who is eternally begotten, in the Holy Spirit, the uncreated person who proceeds from the Father and the Son as their eternal love.

Thus in the three divine persons, *coaeternae sibi et coaequales,* the life and beatitude of God perfectly one superabound and are consummated in the supreme excellence and glory proper to uncreated being, and always "there should be venerated unity in the Trinity and Trinity in the unity."

We believe in Our Lord Jesus Christ, who is the Son of God. He is the Eternal Word, born of the Father before time began, and one in substance with the Father, *homoousios to Patri,* and through him all things were made.

HE WAS incarnate of the Virgin Mary by the power of the Holy Spirit, and was made man: equal therefore to the Father according to his divinity, and inferior to the Father according to his humanity, and himself one, not by some impossible confusion of his natures, but by the unity of his person.

He dwelt among us, full of grace and truth. He proclaimed and established the Kingdom of God and made us know in himself the Father. He gave us his new commandment to love one another as he loved us. He taught us the way of the beatitudes of the Gospel: poverty in spirit, meekness, suffering borne with patience, thirst after justice, mercy, purity of heart, will for peace, persecution suffered for justice sake.

Under Pontius Pilate he suffered, the Lamb of God, bearing on himself the sins of the world, and he died for us on the cross, saving us by his redeeming blood. He was buried and, of his own power, rose the third day, raising us by his Resurrection to that sharing in the divine life which is the life of grace.

He ascended to heaven, and he will come again, this time in glory, to judge the living and the dead: each according to his merits—those who have responded to the love and piety of God going to eternal life, those who have refused them to the end going to the fire that is not extinguished.

AND HIS Kingdom will have no end.

We believe in the Holy Spirit, who is lord, and giver of life, who is adored and glorified together with the Father and the Son. He spoke to us by the Prophets; he was sent by Christ after his Resurrection and his ascension to the Father; he illuminates, vivifies, protects and guides the Church; he purifies the Church's members if they do not shun his grace. His action, which penetrates to the inmost of the soul, enables man to respond to the call of Jesus: Be perfect as your Heavenly Father is perfect (Mt 5, 48).

We believe that Mary is the Mother, who remained ever a Virgin, of the Incarnate Word, our God and Savior Jesus Christ, and that by reason of this singular election, she was, in consideration of the merits of her Son, redeemed in a more eminent manner, preserved from all stain of original sin and filled with the gift of grace more than all other creatures.

Joined by a close and indissoluble bond to the Mysteries of the Incarnation and Redemption, the Blessed Virgin, the Immaculate, was at the end of her earthly life raised body and soul to heavenly glory and likened to her risen Son in anticipation of the future lot of all the just; and we believe that the blessed mother of God, the new Eve, mother of the Church, continues, in heaven her maternal role with regard to Christ's members, cooperating with the birth and growth of divine life in the souls of the redeemed.

WE BELIEVE that in Adam all have sinned, which means that the original offense committed by him caused human nature, common to all men, to fall to a state in which it bears the consequences of that offense, and which is not the state in which it was at first in our first parents, established as they were in holiness and justice, and in which man knew neither evil nor death.

It is human nature so fallen, stripped of the

grace that clothed it, injured in its own natural powers and subjected to the dominion of death, that is transmitted to all, and it is in this sense that every one is born in sin. We therefore hold, with the Council of Trent, that original sin, is transmitted with human nature, "not by imitation, but by propagation" and that it is thus "proper to everyone."

We believe that Our Lord Jesus Christ, by the sacrifice of the cross redeemed us from original sin and all the personal sins committed by each one of us, so that, in accordance with the word of the Apostle, "where sin abounded, grace did more abound."

We believe in one Baptism instituted by Our Lord Jesus Christ for the remission of sins. Baptism should be administered even to little children who have not yet been able to be guilty of any personal sin, in order that, though born deprived of supernatural grace, they may be reborn "of water and the Holy Spirit" to the divine life in Christ Jesus.

WE BELIEVE in one, holy, catholic, and apostolic Church, built by Jesus Christ on that rock which is Peter. She is the Mystical Body of Christ; at the same time a visible society instituted with hierarchical organs, and a spiritual community; the Church on earth, the pilgrim People of God here below, and the Church filled with heavenly blessings; the germ and the first fruits of the Kingdom of God, through which the work and the sufferings of Redemption are continued throughout human history, and which looks for its perfect accomplishment beyond time in glory.

In the course of time, the Lord Jesus forms his Church by means of the sacraments emanating from his plenitude. By these she makes her members participants in the mystery of the Death and Resurrection of Christ, in the grace of the Holy Spirit who gives her life and movement.

She is therefore holy, though she has sinners in her bosom, because she herself has no other life but that of grace: it is by living by her life that her members are sanctified; it is by removing themselves from her life that they fall into sins and disorders that prevent the radiation of her sanctity.

This is why she suffers and does penance for these offenses, of which she has the power to heal her children through the blood of Christ and the gift of the Holy Spirit.

HEIRESS of the divine promises and

daughter of Abraham according to the Spirit, through that Israel whose Scriptures she lovingly guards, and whose Patriarchs and Prophets she venerates; founded upon the Apostles and handing on from century to century their ever-living word and their powers as pastors in the Successor of Peter and the bishops in communion with him; perpetually assisted by the Holy Spirit, she has the charge of guarding, teaching, explaining and spreading the truth which God revealed in a then veiled manner by the Prophets, and fully by the Lord Jesus.

We believe all that is contained in the Word of God written or handed down, and that the Church proposes for belief as divinely revealed, whether by a solemn judgment or by the ordinary and universal magisterium.

We believe in the infallibility enjoyed by the Successor of Peter when he teaches *ex cathedra* as pastor and teacher of all the faithful, and which is assured also to the Episcopal body when it exercises with him the supreme magisterium.

We believe that the Church founded by Jesus Christ and for which he prayed is indefectibly one in faith, worship and the bond of hierarchical communion. In the bosom of this Church, the rich variety of liturgical rites and the legitimate diversity of theological and spiritual heritages and special disciplines, far from injuring her unity, make it more manifest.

RECOGNIZING also the existence, outside the organism of the Church of Christ, of numerous elements of truth and sanctification which belong to her as her own and tend to Catholic unity, and believing in the action of the Holy Spirit who stirs up in the heart of the disciples of Christ love of this unity, we entertain the hope that the Christians who are not yet in the full communion of the one only Church will one day be reunited in one flock with one only shepherd.

We believe that the Church is necessary for salvation, because Christ, who is the sole mediator and way of salvation, renders himself present for us in his Body which is the Church. But the divine design of salvation embraces all; and those who without fault on their part do not know the gospel of Christ and his Church, but seek God sincerely, and under the influence of grace endeavor to do his will as recognized through the promptings of their conscience, they, in a number known only to

God, can obtain salvation.

We believe that the Mass, celebrated by the priest representing the person of Christ by virtue of the power received through the sacrament of Orders, and offered by him in the name of Christ and the members of his Mystical Body, is the sacrifice of Calvary rendered sacramentally present on our altars.

We believe that as the bread and wine consecrated by the Lord at the Last Supper were changed into his Body and his Blood which were to be offered for us on the cross, likewise the bread and wine consecrated by the priest are changed into the Body and Blood of Christ enthroned gloriously in heaven, and we believe that the mysterious presence of the Lord, under what continues to appear to our senses as before, is a true, real and substantial presence.

CHRIST cannot be thus present in this sacrament except by the change into his Body of the reality itself of the bread and the change into his Blood of the reality itself of the wine, leaving unchanged only the properties of the bread and wine which our senses perceive. This mysterious change is very appropriately called by the Church "transubstantiation."

Every theological explanation which seeks some understanding of this mystery must, in order to be in accord with Catholic faith, maintain that in the reality itself, independently of our mind, the bread and wine have ceased to exist after the consecration, so that it is the adorable Body and Blood of the Lord Jesus that from then on are really before us under the sacramental species of bread and wine, as the Lord willed it, in order to give himself to us as food and to associate us with the unity of his Mystical Body.

The unique and indivisible existence of the Lord glorious in heaven is not multiplied, but is rendered present by the sacrament in the many places on earth where Mass is celebrated. And this existence remains present, after the sacrifice, in the Blessed Sacrament which is, in the tabernacle, the living heart of each of our churches. And it is our very sweet duty to honor and adore in the Blessed Host which our eyes see, the Incarnate Word whom they cannot see, and who, without leaving heaven, is made present before us.

WE CONFESS that the Kingdom of God begun here below in the Church of Christ is not of this world whose form is passing, and that its proper growth cannot be confounded with the progress of civilization, of science or of human technology, but that it consists in an ever more profound knowledge of the unfathomable riches of Christ, an ever stronger hope in eternal blessings, an ever more ardent response to the love of God, and an ever more generous bestowal of grace and holiness among men.

But it is this same love which induces the Church to concern herself constantly about the true temporal welfare of all. Without ceasing to recall to her children that they have not here a lasting dwelling, she also urges them to contribute, each according to his vocation and his means, to the welfare of their earthly city, to promote justice, peace and brotherhood among men and women, to give their aid freely to their brothers and sisters especially to the poorest and most unfortunate.

The deep solicitude of the Church, the Spouse of Christ, for the needs of men and women, for their joys and hopes, their griefs and efforts, is therefore nothing other than her great desire to be present to them, in order to illuminate them with the light of Christ and to gather them all in him, their only Savior. This solicitude can never mean that the Church conform herself to the things of this world, or that she lessen the ardor of her expectation of her Lord and of the eternal Kingdom.

We believe in the life eternal. We believe that the souls of all those who die in the grace of Christ, whether they must still be purified in purgatory, or whether from the moment they leave their bodies Jesus takes them to paradise as he did for the good thief, are the people of God in the eternity beyond death, which will be finally conquered on the day of the Resurrection when these souls will be reunited with their bodies.

WE BELIEVE that the multitude of those gathered around Jesus and Mary in paradise forms the Church of heaven, where in eternal beatitude they see God as he is, and where they also, in different degrees, are associated with the holy angels in the divine rule exercised by Christ in glory, interceding for us and helping our weakness by their care.

We believe in the communion of all the faithful of Christ, those who are pilgrims on earth, the dead who are attaining their purification, and the blessed in heaven, all together forming one Church; and we believe that in this communion the merciful love of God and his saints is ever listening to our prayers, as Jesus told us: Ask and you will receive. Thus it is with faith and in hope that we look forward to the resurrection of the dead, and the life of the world to come.

Blessed be God thrice holy. Amen.

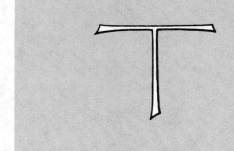

# LITURGICAL PRAYER

# Liturgical Prayer of
# the Secular Franciscan

Article 8 of the Rule of the Secular Franciscan Order states:

"As Jesus was the true worshipper of the Father, so let prayer and contemplation be the soul of all they are and do.

"Let them participate in the sacramental life of the Church, above all the Eucharist. Let them join in liturgical prayer in one of the forms proposed by the Church, reliving the mysteries of the life of Christ."

Following the Sacrament of Reconciliation and Holy Mass, we take up the requirement to pray with and for the Church in one of the forms proposed which may be fulfilled in one of the following ways:

1. Praying Morning and Evening Prayer from the Liturgy of the Hours (Divine Office) privately or with others. (This is the preferred prayer at fraternity meetings.)

2. Praying a shortened form of the Liturgy of the Hours in one of the various styles available today.

3. Praying the "Little Office of the Blessed Virgin." (Unfortunately, this form is not available in a revised format which corresponds with the Divine Office.)

4. Praying the "Office of the Passion" authored by Francis of Assisi, and found in the various collections of the writings of St. Francis.

5. Praying the "Office of the Twelve Our Fathers," which is considered the "traditional" Office of the Secular Franciscans. Many forms of this Office are available which have been adapted to follow the form of the Liturgy of the Hours, and to which have been added short scriptural readings and meditations. This form is and has been widely used because of its adaptability to daily life.

6. One's spiritual director or the fraternity's spiritual assistant may approve another

liturgical prayer form for individual use provided that it contains psalms, biblical readings and prayers.

7. Other prayer forms that correspond to the various liturgical seasons may be substituted from time to time but not on a regular basis, provided that it follows to some extent the form of the liturgical Hours.

# THE SACRAMENT OF PENANCE
## Introduction

In the sacrament of penance or reconciliation we meet Christ the Lord from whom we receive not only forgiveness of sin but also his love and mercy to help us become more Christian—more Christlike.

All sin is basically a failure to love. In the celebration of the sacrament of reconciliation lost love is restored and weakened love is strengthened.

Sin is never a merely private affair. Every sin disrupts the community of the People of God. When one Christian fails to become what he can be, others, too, fail to become what they can be. In this sacrament, therefore, we are reconciled not only to God, but also to the community of the faithful—all of whom have been hurt by our sins.

True reconciliation with God and man is worked out in daily living. Thus the priest may impose a penance appropriate to the sin confessed which can help the sinner move forward along the path of love. Furthermore, the thoughts that the priest might present are offered to encourage and to assist the sinner to "put on the Lord, Jesus Christ."

Some today prefer a "face-to-face" confession. Others desire a more extended discussion of ways to grow in the faith, approaches toward the solution to various problems, or other personal matters. Feel free to ask to talk with a priest.

## 1. Preparation for Receiving the Sacrament of Penance:

A. The following Scripture passage may be read:

"On the evening of that first day of the week, even though the disciples had locked the doors of the place where they were for fear of the Jews, Jesus came and stood before them. 'Peace be with you,' he said. When he had said this, he showed them his hands and his side.

At the sight of the Lord the disciples rejoiced. 'Peace be with you,' he said again. 'As the Father has sent me, so I send you.' Then he breathed on them and said: 'Receive the Holy Spirit. If you forgive men's sins, they are forgiven them; if you hold them bound, they are held bound' " (John 20:19-23).

B. The following psalm verses may be prayed:

In you, O Lord, I take refuge; let me never be put to shame.

In your justice rescue me, incline your ear to me, make haste to deliver me!

Be my rock of refuge, a stronghold to give me safety. You are my rock and fortress;

For your name's sake you will lead and guide me.

I will rejoice and be glad in your kindness, when you have seen my affliction.

Into your hands I commend my spirit; you will redeem me, O Lord, O faithful God (Psalm 31).

C. Prayer before Confession:

O my God, I believe in you. O my God, I hope in you. O my God, I love you above all things. I adore you, here truly present, with all the angels and saints.

I am a poor creature who is not worthy to pray to you. But remembering your infinite goodness, I come to you with the greatest confidence. Give me grace to know my sins, to be heartily sorry for them, to make a sincere confession of them, to obtain forgiveness of them, to sin no more.

O Holy Spirit, who came down upon the Apostles, come down upon me too at this all-important moment. Help me to make a good confession and to be reconciled to God.

And you, O holy Mary, my sweet Mother, behold me here at your feet, and obtain for me forgiveness from my God.

D. Examination of Conscience:

## The Ten Commandments

1. I, the Lord, am your God. You shall not have other gods besides me.
2. You shall not take the name of the Lord, your God, in vain.
3. Remember to keep holy the sabbath day.
4. Honor your father and your mother.
5. You shall not kill.
6. You shall not commit adultery.
7. You shall not steal.
8. You shall not bear false witness against your neighbor.

9. You shall not covet your neighbor's wife.
10. You shall not covet anything that belongs to your neighbor.

## Some Duties of Catholics,
### (Precepts of the Church)*

To keep holy the day of the Lord's resurrection: to worship God by participating in Mass every Sunday and Holy Day of Obligation; to avoid those activities that would hinder renewal of soul and body, e.g., needless work and business activities, unnecessary shopping, etc.

To lead a sacramental life: to receive Holy Communion frequently and the sacrament of penance regularly.

—minimally, to receive the sacrament of penance at least once a year (annual confession is obligatory only if serious sin is involved);

—minimally, to receive Holy Communion at least once a year, between the first Sunday of Lent and Trinity Sunday.

---

*Taken from the Document, *Basic Teachings for Catholic Religious Education,* © 1973, National Conference of Catholic Bishops.

To study Catholic teaching in preparation for the sacrament of confirmation, to be confirmed, and then to continue to study and advance the cause of Christ.

To observe the marriage laws of the Church: to give religious training (by example and word) to one's children; to use parish schools and religious education programs.

To strengthen and support the Church: one's own parish community and parish priests; the worldwide Church and the Holy Father.

To do penance, including abstaining from meat and fasting from food on the appointed days.

### Relationship with God:

— Have I been superstitious to the point of attributing divine powers to created things?
— Have I used the name of God in vain?
— Have I worshipped God as I should both as an individual (by personal prayer) and as a member of the Christian community (by participating actively in the liturgy)?
— Have I been completely negligent in praying to God?

## Regarding Myself:

— Have I continually preferred material things to spiritual values? How does this manifest itself?

— Have I been deliberately impure in thought or deed?

— Have I injured my health by the misuse of food, drugs, or alcohol?

— How well have I used the talents God has given me?

— Have I made positive efforts to grow as a Christian through faith, hope, and love, so that others are able to see Christ in me?

— Am I aware that my life as a Christian is a life of service to others?

## Relationship to Others:

— Do I assume an active responsibility for the life of my parish or do I leave it to others?

— Have I been disrespectful, sarcastic, or critical toward those whom I should respect and love in a special way: my parents, my children, husband or wife, relatives or friends?

— Have I condemned others unjustly or made rash judgments?

— Have I judged others merely on the basis of their race, creed or color? Even hated them?
— Have I harmed another person physically, spiritually, or in any other way by word or deed?
— Have I committed sins of impurity with another?
— Have I acted as a responsible Christian in my marriage?
— Have I attempted to make my marriage grow?
— Have I seen to the Catholic instruction of those over whom God has given me responsibility?
— Have I stolen, cheated or helped others to do these things? Have I kept or accepted stolen goods?
— Have I in any way hurt the good name or reputation of any person or community?
— Have I neglected to help those who need my help: the sick, the aged, the lonely, the poor?
— Have I hurt others by my bad example?
— Have I tried to spread the peace of Christ at home, at work, in the community?

E. Arouse in yourself sorrow for your sins and make a sincere act of contrition.

*(It is recommended that this act of contrition be prayed before entering the confessional. This may be done either in your own words or in the traditional formula.)*

O my God, I am heartily sorry for having offended you, and I detest all my sins, because of your punishments, but most of all because they offend you, my God, who are all-good and deserving of all my love. I firmly resolve, with the help of your grace, to sin no more and to avoid the occasions of sin.

F. Things to Remember:

All serious sins are to be confessed along with the number of times. If the number of times is not known, an approximation is sufficient.

If there are no serious sins to be confessed, you may:

(a) confess venial sins—numbers are not necessary;

(b) or confess some sins of the past;

(c) or simply say, "I am sorry for all the sins of my past life";

(d) or mention any special area in your life

wherein you commonly fail.

Do not confess things that are not sins such as missing Mass because of illness; missing morning or night prayer; unwillful distractions in prayer; temptations, etc.

## II. The Confession Itself
### (according to the New Rite of Penance)

After the priest has welcomed you, make the sign of the cross and say: "In the name of the Father, and of the Son, and of the Holy Spirit. Amen."

The priest invites you to have trust in God, and you answer: "Amen."

The priest may read or quote a short excerpt from Holy Scripture.

You then confess the sins which you have committed—at least all grievous sins. The priest will help you to make an integral confession, give you suitable counsel, and propose an act of penance which you accept to make satisfaction for sin and to amend your life.

After the priest has asked you to do so, express your sorrow for your sins, using a formula you know or your own words.

The priest extends his hands or his right hand and absolves you from your sins, saying:

**"God, the Father of mercies,
through the death and resurrection of his Son
has reconciled the world to himself
and sent the Holy Spirit among us
for the forgiveness of sins;
through the ministry of the Church
may God give you pardon and peace,
and I absolve you from your sins
in the name of the Father and of the Son, †
and of the Holy Spirit."**

You answer: "Amen."

The priest continues: "Give thanks to the Lord, for he is good." And you respond: "His mercy endures for ever."

The priest dismisses you with the words: "The Lord has freed you from your sins. Go in peace!" or some other prayerful farewell.

## III. Prayer after Absolution:

After confession you may wish to pray the following psalm:

The Lord is my shepherd; I shall not want.

In verdant pastures he gives me repose;

Beside restful waters he leads me; he refreshes my soul.

He guides me in right paths for his name's sake.

Even though I walk in the dark valley I fear no evil; for you are at my side with your rod and your staff that give me courage.

You spread the table before me in the sight of my foes;

You anoint my head with oil; my cup overflows.

Only goodness and kindness follow me all the days of my life;

And I shall dwell in the house of the Lord for years to come (Psalm 23).

## IV. Prayer of Thanksgiving:

O most merciful God, who, according to the multitude of your tender mercies, have received once more your prodigal child, after so often going astray; I give you thanks with all the powers of my soul for this and all other mercies, graces, and blessings bestowed on me, and, prostrating myself at your sacred feet, I offer myself to be henceforth forever yours. Oh, let nothing in life or death ever separate me from you! I renounce with my whole soul all my treasons against you and all sins of my past life. I renew my promises made in baptism, and from this moment I dedicate myself eternally to your love and service. Oh, grant that for the time to come I may abhor sin more than death itself, and avoid all such occasions as have unhappily brought me to it. This I resolve to do by the aid of your divine grace, without which I can do nothing. I beg your blessing upon these my resolutions, that they may be not ineffectual, like so many others I have made; for, O Lord, without you I am nothing but misery and sin. Supply, also, by your mercy, whatever defects I may have committed in this confession, and give me grace to be now and always a true penitent. Through the same Jesus Christ, your Son.—Amen.

## HOLY MASS

"The sacred liturgy does not exhaust the entire activity of the Church . . . Nevertheless the liturgy is the summit toward which the activity of the Church is directed; at the same time it is the font from which all her power flows. For the aim and object of apostolic works is that all who are made sons of God by faith and baptism should come together to praise God in the midst of his Church, to take part in the sacrifice, and to eat the Lord's supper . . .

"But in order that the liturgy may be able to produce its full effects, it is necessary that the faithful come to it with proper dispositions, that their minds should be attuned to their voices, and that they should cooperate with divine grace lest they receive it in vain . . .

"Mother Church earnestly desires that all the faithful should be led to that full, conscious, and active participation in liturgical celebrations which is demanded by the very nature of the liturgy . . .

"The Church, therefore, earnestly desires that Christ's faithful, when present at this mystery of faith (the Holy Sacrifice of the Mass), should not be there as strangers or silent spectators; on the contrary, through a good understanding of the rites and prayers, they should take part in the sacred action, conscious of what they are doing, with devotion and full collaboration.

"They should be instructed by God's word and be nourished at the table of the Lord's Body, they should give thanks to God; by offering the Immaculate Victim, not only through the hands of the priest, but also with him, they should learn also to offer themselves; through Christ the mediator, they should be drawn day by day into ever more perfect union with God and with each other, so that finally God may be all in all" (*Constitution on the Sacred Liturgy,* nos. 9, 10, 11, 14, 48).

**ENGLISH TEXT OF THE
ORDINARY PARTS PERTAINING
TO THE PEOPLE**

## Introductory Rites

**Entrance Song**           **STAND**

(*As the priest and the ministers approach the altar, all stand and sing the Entrance Song: A) a Hymn, or B) a Seasonal Antiphon and Psalm or C) the Entrance Antiphon and Psalm for the day.*)

## Greeting

**Celebrant:** In the name of the Father, and of the Son, and of the Holy Spirit.

**PEOPLE:** Amen.

**Celebrant:** The grace of our Lord Jesus Christ and the love of God and the fellowship of the Holy Spirit be with you all.

*or*

The grace and peace of God our Father and the Lord Jesus Christ be with you.

*or*

**The Lord be with you.**

**PEOPLE:** And also with you.

---

### Penitential Rite

**Celebrant:** My brothers and sisters, to prepare ourselves to celebrate the sacred mysteries, let us call to mind our sins.

(*One of the following forms of the Penitential Prayer is recited.*)

Form A

**ALL:** I confess to almighty God, and to you, my brothers and sisters, that I have sinned through my own fault in my thoughts and in my words, in what I have done, and in what I have failed to do: and I ask blessed Mary, ever virgin, all the angels and saints, and you, my brothers and sisters, to pray for me to the Lord our God.

Form B

**Celebrant:** Lord, we have sinned against you:
Lord, have mercy.

**PEOPLE:** Lord, have mercy.

**Celebrant:** Lord, show us your mercy and love.

**PEOPLE:** And grant us your salvation.

Form C

You were sent to heal the contrite:
Lord, have mercy.

**PEOPLE:** Lord, have mercy.

**Celebrant:** You came to call sinners:
Christ, have mercy.

**PEOPLE:** Christ, have mercy.

**Celebrant:** You plead for us at the right hand
of the Father:
Lord, have mercy.

**PEOPLE:** Lord, have mercy.

**Celebrant:** My almighty God have mercy on
us, forgive us our sins, and bring us
to everlasting life. Amen.

## Litany of Mercy

(*If Form C was used, omit the Litany of Mercy.*)

**Celebrant:** Lord, have mercy.

**PEOPLE:** Lord, have mercy.

**Celebrant:** Christ, have mercy.

| PEOPLE: | Christ, have mercy. |
| **Celebrant:** | Lord, have mercy. |
| **PEOPLE:** | Lord, have mercy. |

## Glory to God

**ALL:** Glory to God in the highest, and peace to his people on earth.

Lord God, heavenly King, almighty God and Father, we worship you, we give you thanks, we praise you for your glory.

Lord Jesus Christ, only Son of the Father, Lord God, Lamb of God, you take away the sin of the world: have mercy on us; you are seated at the right hand of the Father: receive our prayer.

For you alone are the Holy One, you alone are the Lord, you alone are the Most High, Jesus Christ, with the Holy Spirit, in the glory of God the Father. Amen.

## Prayer of the Day

**Celebrant:** Let us pray.
(*At the conclusion of the prayer—*)
**PEOPLE:** Amen.

## Lessons and Responses                    SIT

(*At the conclusion of the reading—*)
**Lector:**     This is the Word of the Lord.
**PEOPLE:**     Thanks be to God.

## Gospel Acclamation        STAND

**Deacon (or Priest):** The Lord be with you.
**ALL:**                And also with you.
**Deacon (or Priest):** † A reading from the holy
                        gospel according to . . .
**ALL:**                Glory to you, Lord.
(*At the conclusion of the Gospel—*)
**Deacon (or Priest):** This is the gospel of the
                        Lord.
**ALL:**                Praise to you, Lord Jesus
                        Christ.

## Homily              SIT

## Creed              STAND

**ALL:**    We believe in one God, the Father,
            the Almighty, maker of heaven and
            earth, of all that is seen and unseen.
            We believe in one Lord, Jesus
            Christ, the only Son of God,
            eternally begotten of the Father,
            God from God, Light from Light,
            true God from true God, begotten,

not made, one in Being with the Father. Through him all things were made. For us men and for our salvation he came down from heaven: by the power of the Holy Spirit.

(*All bow at the following words up to: and became man.*)

he was born of the Virgin Mary, and became man. For our sake he was crucified under Pontius Pilate; he suffered, died, and was buried. On the third day he rose again in fulfillment of the Scriptures; he ascended into heaven and is seated at the right hand of the Father. He will come again in glory to judge the living and the dead, and his kingdom will have no end. We believe in the Holy Spirit, the Lord, the giver of life, who proceeds from the Father and the Son. With the Father and the Son he is worshiped and glorified. He has spoken through the Prophets. We believe in one holy catholic and apostolic Church. We acknowledge one baptism for the forgiveness of sins. We look for the resurrection of the dead, and the life of the world to come. Amen.

## General Intercession

**Celebrant:** Let us pray.
(*The priest may develop his invitation to pray through a sentence related to the day's liturgy. After each petition add:* Let us pray to the Lord.)
*One of the responses will be assigned.*

1. We hope in you.
2. Grant this, O Lord.
3. We ask you, Lord.
4. Lord, answer us.

(*All pause for silent prayer. Then the celebrant sings or recites a concluding prayer.*)
**ALL:** Amen. **SIT**

# LITURGY OF THE EUCHARIST
## Preparation of the Gifts

(*The Eucharistic People of God celebrate their redemption by offering gifts for the banquet of the Lord and contributions for those in need.*)

## Processional Song

(*While the gifts are collected and brought to*

*the altar, A) a Processional Hymn, or B) a Seasonal Antiphon and Psalm or C) the Offertory Verse for the day may be sung: thus, the common unity of all God's people is heralded.)*

### Offertory Prayers

**Celebrant:** Blessed are you, Lord, God of all creation. Through your goodness we have this bread to offer, which earth has given and human hands have made. It will become for us the bread of life.

**PEOPLE:** Blessed be God forever.

**Celebrant:** Blessed are you, Lord, God of all creation. Through your goodness we have this wine to offer, fruit of the vine and work of human hands. It will become our spiritual drink.

**PEOPLE:** Blessed be God forever.

### Petition for Prayer

**Celebrant:** Pray, brethren, that our sacrifice may be acceptable to God, the almighty Father.

**PEOPLE:** May the Lord accept the sacrifice at your hands for the praise and glory of his name, for our good, and the good of all his Church.

### Prayer over the Gifts

**Celebrant:** Let us pray.       **STAND**
(*At the conclusion of the prayer—*)
**PEOPLE:** Amen.

# The Eucharistic Prayer

**Celebrant:** The Lord be with you.
**PEOPLE:** And also with you.
**Celebrant:** Lift up your hearts.
**PEOPLE:** We lift them up to the Lord.
**Celebrant:** Let us give thanks to the Lord our God.
**PEOPLE:** It is right to give him thanks and praise.

### Preface

(*In the Preface the celebrant expresses the particular reasons for our thanks to the Father at this Mass. At the conclusion of the Preface.*)

### Holy, Holy

**ALL:** Holy, holy, holy Lord, God of power and might, heaven and earth are full of your glory. Hosanna in the highest. Blessed is he who comes

in the name of the Lord. Hosanna
in the highest.

**KNEEL**

### Memorial Acclamation

**Celebrant:** Let us proclaim the mystery of
faith:

**ALL:** (One of these)

1. Christ has died,
   Christ is risen,
   Christ will come again.
2. Dying you destroyed our death,
   rising you restored our life.
   Lord Jesus, come in glory.
3. When we eat this bread and drink
   this cup, we proclaim your death,
   Lord Jesus, until you come in glory.
4. Lord, by your cross and resurrection, you have set us free.
   You are the Savior of the world.

### Great Amen

**Priest:** Through him, with him, in him, in
the unity of the Holy Spirit, all glory
and honor is yours, almighty Father,
forever and ever.

**ALL:** Amen.

# Communion Rite

## The Lord's Prayer

**STAND**

**Celebrant:** Let us pray with confidence to the Father in the words our Savior gave us:

**PRIEST AND PEOPLE:** Our Father who art in heaven, *hallowed be thy name; *thy kingdom come; *thy will be done on earth as it is in heaven. *Give us this day our daily bread: *and forgive us our trespasses *as we forgive those who trespass against us; *and lead us not into temptation, *but deliver us from evil.*

## Prayer for Peace

**Celebrant:** Deliver us, Lord, from every evil, and grant us peace in our day. In your mercy keep us free from sin and protect us from all anxiety as we wait in joyful hope for the coming of our Savior, Jesus Christ.

**PEOPLE:** For the kingdom, the power, and the glory are yours, now and forever.

## Prayer for Unity

**Celebrant:** Lord Jesus Christ, you said to your apostles: I leave you peace, my peace I give you. Look not on our sins, but on the faith of your Church, and grant us the peace and unity of your kingdom where you live forever and ever.

**PEOPLE:** Amen.

**Celebrant:** The peace of the Lord be with you always.

**PEOPLE:** And also with you.

## Sign of Peace

**Celebrant:** Let us offer each other the sign of peace.

*(All, according to local custom, make an appropriate gesture of peace and charity toward one another, using their own words or the following:)*

**PEOPLE:** The Lord's peace be with you.

## Lamb of God

**ALL:** Lamb of God, you take away the sins of the world: have mercy on us. Lamb of God, you take away the sins of the world: have mercy on us.

Lamb of God, you take away the
sins of the world: grant us peace.

**KNEEL**

## Communion of the Faithful

**Celebrant:** This is the Lamb of God who takes
away the sins of the world. Happy
are those who are called to his
supper.

**ALL:** (once only): Lord, I am not worthy
to receive you, but only say the
word and I shall be healed.

**Celebrant:** The body of Christ.
**COMMUNICANT:** Amen.
(When receiving under both species)
**Celebrant:** The blood of Christ.
**COMMUNICANT:** Amen.

## Communion Song

(*During the distribution of Communion the
people may sing; A) a Hymn, or B) the Seasonal
Antiphon and Psalm or C) the Communion
Verse for the day.*)

## Period of Common Thanksgiving

**SIT**

(*Before the Prayer after Communion, a period*

*of silence may be observed and/or a Post-communion song, psalm, or canticle of praise may be recited or sung. The Litany of Thanksgiving may be used at this time.)*

### Prayer after Communion

**Celebrant:** Let us pray.

**STAND**

*(At the conclusion of the prayer—)*
**PEOPLE:** Amen.

## Dismissal Rite

**Celebrant:** The Lord be with you.
**PEOPLE:** And also with you.
**Celebrant:** May almighty God bless you, the Father, and the Son, † and the Holy Spirit.
**PEOPLE:** Amen.
**Deacon (or Celebrant):** Go in the peace of Christ. (Alleluia, alleluia.)

*or*

The Mass is ended, go in peace. (Alleluia, alleluia.)

*or*

Go in peace to love and serve the Lord. (Alleluia, alleluia.)

**PEOPLE:** Thanks be to God. (Alleluia. Alleluia)

### Recessional Song

*(As the priest and ministers leave the altar, a concluding song may be sung.)*

\*　　\*　　\*

O Virgin Mary, our Lady of the Blessed Sacrament, glory of the Christian people, joy of the universal Church, salvation of the whole world, pray for us, and awaken in all believers a lively devotion to the Most Holy Eucharist, that so they may be made worthy to partake of It daily.

# ALTERNATE FORMS OF OFFICE

## FOREWORD

"REJOICE ALWAYS, NEVER CEASE praying, render constant thanks; such is God's will for you in Christ Jesus" (1 Thes. 5:16-18).

Since the Franciscan Way of Life is a vital part of the life and growth of the Church, those who embrace this Way unite themselves with all others who carry the responsibility of praying with and for the Church, not only in their own private manner, but in an official capacity. Hence, the Franciscans' participation in the Liturgy of the Hours (or Divine Office) becomes an important element of their charism and mission.

It is fully recognized that the new English

breviary which is the official translation of the Church's normative text for the Liturgy of the Hours is the most ideal way for the Franciscans to join in the official on-going prayer of the whole Church. However, because of various extenuating circumstances (whether time or place or unavailability of the official text or lack of familiarity with its use) the ideal cannot always be fulfilled to the letter. Yet the spirit of praying in an official way with all the members of the Church still remains. Hence, because of necessity or custom other similar forms of "Divine Office" have arisen over the years to take care of this responsibility and desire intensely felt by the Franciscans.

From the earliest days of the Franciscan Order the tradition had arisen that the lay members of the community be permitted to pray the Our Fathers as a way of fulfilling their responsibility to join in the official prayer of the Church. In the earliest extant Third Order Rule and in the Rule of Leo XIII the Divine Office of the Our Fathers is mentioned and recommended.

Even though the liturgical style of prayer is more strongly encouraged, still the Our Father Office is a very important aspect of the Franciscan tradition and should be rightly considered.

Attention therefore is given here to various forms of the Our Father Office which have become popular over the years. The form of the Offices given here has been slightly altered to comply with the nature of the Liturgy of the Hours and with the directives of the Church. The options presented for the traditional Twelve Our Father Office can be used according to the discretion of the fraternity and/or the individual.

Keep in mind, however, that to preserve the true character of the special times of prayer (morning and evening), all effort should be made to say the given prayer at the appropriate time of the day, rather than saying the whole office at one time either alone or in common. It is a violation of the spirit of the Liturgy of the Hours, for example, to say the **whole** Office of the Passion, Seraphic Office, etc., at the monthly fraternity meeting. (Cf. the July, 1974, issue of the *Franciscan Herald* magazine, entitled "Implementing the 'New Ritual for Public Functions,' Part 6: The Lay Franciscans and the Divine Office," pp. 218-222.)

This text will provide some sort of constancy

for the Franciscans' participation in the Liturgy of the Hours, but at the same time will be open-ended enough to preserve and promote the grass-roots initiative of all praying Franciscans. This handbook is intended to organize the methods of praying the Liturgy of the Hours for Franciscans as well as give them an easy reference for variety and style in their official prayer with the Church.

"We must love God, then, and adore him with a pure heart and mind, because this is what he seeks above all else, as he tells us, 'True worshippers will worship the Father in spirit and in truth' (Jn 4:23). All 'who worship him must worship him in spirit and in truth' (Jn 4:24). We should praise him and pray to him day and night, saying 'Our Father, who art in heaven' (Mt 6:9), because we 'must always pray and not lose heart' (Lk 18:1)." (St. Francis, "Letter to All the Faithful")

BENET A. FONCK O.F.M.

119

## THE LITURGICAL OFFICE OF
## THE TWELVE OUR FATHERS
### Morning Prayer

**V.** In the name of the Father, and of the Son, and of the Holy Spirit.

**R. Amen.**

**V.** Come, let us sing joyfully to the Lord.

**R. Let us acclaim the rock of our salvation.**

**V.** Let us greet him with thanksgiving;

**R. Let us joyfully sing psalms to him.**

*Our Father, Hail Mary, Glory be.*

**V.** For the Lord is a great God;

**R. And a great King above all gods.**

*Our Father, Hail Mary, Glory be.*

**V.** In his hands are the depths of the earth,

**R. And the tops of the mountains are his.**

*Our Father, Hail Mary, Glory be.*

**V.** His is the sea, for he has made it.

**R. And the dry land, which his hands have formed.**

*Our Father, Hail Mary, Glory be.*

**V.** Come, let us bow down in worship;

**R. Let us kneel before the Lord who made us.**

*Our Father, Hail Mary, Glory be.*

**V.** For he is our God

**R. And we are the people he shepherds, the flock he guides.**

(Ps 95:1-7)

*Our Father, Hail Mary, Glory be.*

**V.** Night is on its way and day has drawn near. So let us cast off the works of darkness and put on the armor of light. Let us live decently, as in daylight.

(Rom 13:11) -

**R. Thanks be to God.**

*Our Father, Hail Mary, Glory be.*


Scripture Reading: (*optional*)

| | |
|---|---|
| Sunday | Eph 1:3-4 |
| Monday | 1 John 3:1-3 |
| Tuesday | Rom 8:18-25 |
| Wednesday | I John 4:7-12 |

| Thursday | I Cor 13:1-8 |
| Friday | I John 4:13-17 |
| Saturday | I Cor 15:51-58 |

*Meditation (moment of silent prayer)*

**V.** Let us pray:

**R. O Lord, God almighty, * who have had us reach the beginning of this day; * preserve us today with your power, * so that this day we shall in no manner give way to sin * but that what we say and think and do * may tend and be directed toward promoting your holy will. * Through our Lord Jesus Christ, your Son, * who with you lives and reigns in unity with the Holy Spirit as God, world without end. Amen.**

\* \* \*

### Evening Prayer

**V.** In the name of the Father, and of the Son, and of the Holy Spirit.

**R. Amen.**

**V.** To the King of Ages, the immortal and invisible, who alone is God, be honor and glory world without end.

*(1 Tim 1:17)*

**R. Amen!**

*Our Father, Hail Mary, Glory be.*

**V.** God is love, and whoever abides in love, abides in God and God in him.

*(1 Jn 4:16)*

**R. Amen!**

*Our Father, Hail Mary, Glory be.*

**V.** Let each of you bear the other's burdens, and so you will fulfill the Law of Christ.

*(Gal 6:2)*

**R. Amen!**

*Our Father, Hail Mary, Glory be.*

**V.** You have been bought at a great price. Glorify God and bear him about in your person.

*(1 Cor 6:20)*

**R. Amen!**

*Our Father, Hail Mary, Glory be.*

**V.** The fiery sun now leaves the sky.

**R. Thou, Light eternal Unity
And ever blessed Trinity,
Still light our hearts unendingly.**

*Our Father, Hail Mary, Glory be.*

**V.** Into your hands, O Lord, we commend our spirit.

**R.** **You have redeemed us, O Lord, the God of truth.**

*Our Father, Hail Mary, Glory be.*

Scripture Reading: *(optional)*

| | |
|---|---|
| Sunday | James 1:19-27 |
| Monday | James 2:1-13 |
| Tuesday | James 2:14-26 |
| Wednesday | James 3:1-12 |
| Thursday | James 3:13-18 |
| Friday | James 4:1-12 |
| Saturday | James 5:7-20 |

Meditation *(moment of silent prayer)*

**V.** Let my prayer come like incense before you.

**R.** **The raising of my hands like an evening sacrifice.**

**V.** Let us pray:

**ALL: Defend us, O Lord, we beseech you, * from all dangers of body and soul; * and at the intercession of the glorious and blessed Mary ever virgin Mother of God * and with blessed Joseph, the blessed Apostles Peter and Paul, * our holy father Francis and all the saints, * grant us in your kindness both safety and peace; * so that, with all error and adversity put to**

nought, * your Church may serve you secure in its liberty. * Through our Lord Jesus Christ, your Son, * who with you lives and reigns in unity with the Holy Spirit as God, world without end. Amen.

## OFFICE OF THE PASSION
### Morning Prayer

**V.** In the name of the Father, and of the Son, and of the Holy Spirit.

**R. Amen.**

**V.** O Lord Jesus Christ, who on the eve of your sufferings instituted the Blessed Sacrament.

**R. Have mercy on us.**

*Our Father, Hail Mary, Glory be.*

**V.** O Lord Jesus Christ, who, sorrowful unto death, prayed to your heavenly Father,

**R. Have mercy on us,**

*Our Father, Hail Mary, Glory be.*

**V.** O Lord Jesus Christ, whose sacred body in your agony was bathed in a bloody sweat,

**R. Have mercy on us.**

*Our Father, Hail Mary, Glory be.*

**V.** O Lord Jesus Christ, who, betrayed by

Judas, were taken captive,

**R. Have mercy on us.**

*Our Father, Hail Mary, Glory be.*

**V.** O Lord Jesus Christ, who were led bound to Annas and Caiphas,

**R. Have mercy on us.**

*Our Father, Hail Mary, Glory be.*

**V.** O Lord Jesus Christ, who were declared by the high priest guilty of death,

**R. Have mercy on us.**

*Our Father, Hail Mary, Glory be.*

Scripture Reading: *(optional)*

| | |
|---|---|
| Sunday | John 12:23-28 |
| Monday | Matt 16:21-23 |
| Tuesday | Matt 27:45-61 |
| Wednesday | Mark 15:29-47 |
| Thursday | Luke 23:33-49 |
| Friday | John 19:25-37 |
| Saturday | Mark 10:32-34 |

Meditation *(moment of silent prayer)*

**V.** Let us pray:

**ALL: O God, * who caused the precious body of our blessed father Francis * to be brought forth from darkness to light: ***

**grant us, we beseech you, * to escape from the night of sin * and to direct our steps in the way of peace and justice. * Through Christ our Lord. Amen.**

*       *       *

### Evening Prayer

**V.** In the name of the Father, and of the Son, and of the Holy Spirit.

**R. Amen.**

**V.** O Lord Jesus Christ who at the first hour of the day were delivered up to the heathen judge Pilate,

**R. Have mercy on us.**

*Our Father, Hail Mary, Glory be.*

**V.** O Lord Jesus Christ, who at the third hour were cruelly scourged, and crowned with thorns,

**R. Have mercy on us.**

*Our Father, Hail Mary, Glory be.*

**V.** O Lord Jesus Christ, who at the sixth hour were nailed to the cross with heavy nails,

**R. Have mercy on us.**

*Our Father, Hail Mary, Glory be.*

**V.** O Lord Jesus Christ, who at the ninth hour gave up your spirit into the hands of your Father.

**R. Have mercy on us.**

*Our Father, Hail Mary, Glory be.*

**V.** O Lord Jesus Christ, who at vesper time were taken down from the cross and placed in the arms of your Mother,

**R. Have mercy on us.**

*Our Father, Hail Mary, Glory be.*

**V.** O Lord Jesus Christ, who were borne by your most afflicted Mother and your dearest friends to the tomb,

**R. Have mercy on us.**

*Our Father, Hail Mary, Glory be.*


Scripture Reading: *(optional)*

| | |
|---|---|
| Sunday | Heb 9:11-15 |
| Monday | Heb 5:7-9 |
| Tuesday | II Cor 4:7-14 |
| Wednesday | I Cor 1:18-25 |
| Thursday | Eph 2:13-18 |
| Friday | Phil 2:5-11 |
| Saturday | Phil 3:7-14 |

Meditation *(moment of silent prayer)*

**V.** Let us pray:

**ALL:** **O Lord Jesus Christ, * who, when the world was growing cold, * renewed the sacred marks of your passion in the flesh of the most blessed Francis, * to inflame our hearts with the fire of your love, * mercifully grant that by his merits and prayers * we may always carry the cross * and bring forth worthy fruits of penance, * Through Christ our Lord. Amen.**

# NON–LITURGICAL OFFICES

## THE SERAPHIC OFFICE

### Morning Prayer

**V.** In the name of the Father, and of the Son, and of the Holy Spirit.

**R. Amen.**

**V.** O Lord, open my lips,

**R. And my mouth shall declare your praise.**

**V.** Come, let us adore Christ the King, who exalts the humble.

*Our Father, Hail Mary, Glory be.*

**V.** New signs of highest sanctity,
Deserving praise exceedingly,
Wondrous and beautiful to see,
In Francis we behold.

**R.** **Unto the newly gathered band,**
**Directed by his guiding hand,**
**Francis receives the King's command,**
**The new law to unfold.**

*Our Father, Hail Mary, Glory be.*

**V.** Before the world's astonished view,
Arise the life and order new,
Whose sacred laws again renew
The evangelic state.

**R.** **The rule monastic he reforms,**
**And to the law of Christ conforms,**
**And all the apostolic forms**
**He holds inviolate.**

*Our Father, Hail Mary, Glory be.*

**V.** In raiment coarse and rough endued,
A cord his only cincture rude,
Scanty the measure of his food,
His feet withal unshod.

**R.** **For poverty alone he yearns,**
**From earthly things he loathing turns,**
**The noble Francis money spurns,**
**Despising all for God.**

*Our Father, Hail Mary, Glory be.*

**V.** He seeks a place to weep, apart,
And mourns in bitterness of heart,
Time precious lost when taking part
In earthly joys, and vain.

**R. Within a mountain cavern lone
He hides to weep, and lying prone,
He prays with many a sign and groan
Till calm returns again.**

*Our Father, Hail Mary, Glory be.*

**V.** There, in that rocky cave's retreat,
Rapt high in contemplation sweet,
The earth (wise judge) beneath his feet,
To heaven he aspires.

**R. His flesh by penance is subdued,
Transfigured wholly, and renewed;
The Scriptures are his daily food,
Renouncing earth's desires.**

*Our Father, Hail Mary, Glory be.*

Scripture Reading: *(optional)*

|           | WEEK I        | WEEK II       |
|-----------|---------------|---------------|
| Sunday    | Matt 28:16-20 | Mark 16:14-18 |
| Monday    | Matt 10:7-20  | Mark 6:7-13   |
| Tuesday   | Matt 11:25-30 | Mark 1:14-18  |
| Wednesday | Matt 18:1-4   | Mark 9:33-36  |

| Thursday | Matt 19:13-15 | Mark 10:13-16 |
| Friday | Matt 16:24-27 | Mark 8:34-36 |
| Saturday | Matt 19:16-21 | Mark 10:17-22 |

## WEEK III

| Sunday | Luke 24:44-49 |
| Monday | Luke 9:1-6 |
| Tuesday | Luke 10:21-22 |
| Wednesday | Luke 9:46-47 |
| Thursday | Luke 18:15-17 |
| Friday | Luke 9:23-26 |
| Saturday | Luke 18:18-23 |

Meditation *(moment of quiet prayer)*

**V.** If we have been united with him through likeness to his death,

**R. So shall we be through a like resurrection.**

*(Rom 6:5)*

**V.** Let us pray:

O God, you enable us to walk in the ways of your Son by giving us blessed Francis as a guide and teacher. We ask that we may deserve to share the heavenly glory of him whose memory we celebrate and whose life we imitate. We ask this through Christ our Lord.

**R. Amen.**

\*     \*     \*

## Evening Prayer

**V.** In the name of the Father, and of the Son, and of the Holy Spirit.

**R. Amen.**

**V.** He humbled himself before the Lord who also exalted him.

**R. For God resists the proud but to the humble he gives peace.**

*Our Father, Hail Mary, Glory be.*

**V.** Then Seraph-like in heaven's height
The King of kings appears in sight,
The patriarch, in sore affright,
Beholds the vision dread.

**R. It bears the wounds of Christ, and lo,
While gazing on in speechless woe,
It marks him, and the stigmas show
Upon his flesh, blood-red.**

*Our Father, Hail Mary, Glory be.*

**V.** His body, like the Crucified,
Is signed on hands and feet; his side
Transfixed from right to left, and dyed
With crimson streams of blood.

**R. Unto his mind words secret sound,
Things future all in light abound,
Inspired from on high, the saint has found
Their sense, and understood.**

*Our Father, Hail Mary, Glory be.*

**V.** Now, in those bleeding wounds, behold,
Black nails appear, within all gold;
Sharp are the points, the pain untold,
Unspeakable the woe.

**R. No instrument of man was brought
To make those wounds, here art did naught,
By nature's hand they were not wrought,
Nor cruel mallet blow.**

*Our Father, Hail Mary, Glory be.*

**V.** We pray thee, by the Cross's sign
Marked on thy flesh, whereby 'twas thine
The world, the flesh, the foe malign
To conquer gloriously.

**R. Take us, O Francis, to thy care,
Shield us from woe, from every snare,
That we thy great reward may share
In heaven eternally.**

*Our Father, Hail Mary, Glory be.*

**V.** O father holy, father sweet,
Devoutly we thine aid entreat.
May we and all thy brethren meet,
Victorious in the strife.

**R. In virtue's way our footsteps train,
And bring us with the saints to reign.**

**So may thy flock of children gain
The joys of endless life.
Amen.**

*Our Father, Hail Mary, Glory be.*

Scripture Reading *(optional)*

|           | WEEK I        | WEEK II      |
|-----------|---------------|--------------|
| Sunday    | Acts 2:42-47  | Acts 4:32-35 |
| Monday    | Eph 1:3-14    | Phil 3:7-11  |
| Tuesday   | Rom 10:9-18   | I Cor 1:26-31|
| Wednesday | I Jn 3:14-18  | I Jn 4:7-16  |
| Thursday  | Rom 14:7-11   | Eph 6:10-18  |
| Friday    | Gal 2:19-20   | Gal 6:14-18  |
| Saturday  | I Pet 2:21-25 | 2 Pet 1:3-11 |

|           | WEEK III        |
|-----------|-----------------|
| Sunday    | Acts 10:34-43   |
| Monday    | Col 1:15-20     |
| Tuesday   | 2 Cor 10:17-11:2|
| Wednesday | I Jn 5:1-5      |
| Thursday  | Phil 4:4-9     |
| Friday    | Phil 2:2-11     |
| Saturday  | Jude 20-25      |

Meditation *(moment of quiet prayer)*

**V.** Pray for us, holy Father Francis;

**R. Make us worthy of the promises of Christ.**

**V.** O God, you resist the proud and give grace

to the humble. Grant that through the intercession of our holy Father Francis, we may
not be puffed up with pride but may become more pleasing to you through
humility, so that walking in his footsteps,
we may obtain the gifts of your grace. We
ask this through Christ our Lord.

**R. Amen.**

## THE OFFICE OF PRAISE
### Morning Prayer

**V.** In the name of the Father, and of the Son,
and of the Holy Spirit.

**R. Amen.**

**Leader:** Come, let us sing joyfully to the Lord;
let us acclaim the Rock of our
salvation.

*(Ps 95:1)*

*Our Father . . .*

**Side 1:** **Let us greet him with thanksgiving;
let us joyfully sing psalms to him.**

*(Ps 95:2)*

*Hail Mary . . .*

**Side 2:** Come, let us bow down in worship; let us kneel before the Lord who made us.

*(Ps 95:6)*

*Glory be . . .*

**Leader:** Sing joyfully to the Lord, all you lands; serve the Lord with gladness.

*(Ps 100:1)*

*Our Father . . .*

**Side 1:** Enter his gates with thanksgiving, his courts with praise; Give thanks to him, bless his name.

*(Ps 100:4)*

*Hail Mary . . .*

**Side 2:** Be glad in the Lord, you just, and give thanks to his holy name.

*(Ps 97:12)*

*Glory be . . .*

**Leader:** Sing to the Lord a new song; sing to the Lord, all you lands.

*(Ps 96:1)*

*Our Father . . .*

**Side 1:** Sing to the Lord, bless his name; announce his salvation, day after day.

*(Ps 96:2)*

*Hail Mary . . .*

**Side 2:** **Tell his glory among the nations; among all peoples, his wondrous deeds.**

*(Ps 96:3)*

*Glory be . . .*

**Leader:** Bless the Lord, O my soul; and all my being bless his holy name.

*(Ps 103:1)*

*Our Father . . .*

**Side 1:** **Bless the Lord, O my soul! O Lord, my God, you are great indeed!**

*(Ps 104:1)*

*Hail Mary . . .*

**Side 2:** **Give thanks to the Lord, invoke his name; make known among the nations his deeds.**

*(Ps 105:1)*

*Glory be . . .*

**Leader:** Sing to the Lord a new song, for he has done wondrous deeds; His right hand has won victory for him, his holy arm.

*(Ps 98:1)*

*Our Father . . .*

138

**Side 1:** The Lord has made his salvation known: in the sight of the nations he has revealed his justice.

*(Ps 98:2)*

*Hail Mary . . .*

**Side 2:** He has remembered his kindness and his faithfulness toward the house of Israel.

*(Ps 98:3)*

*Glory be . . .*

**Leader:** Give thanks to the Lord, for he is good, for his kindness endures forever.

*(Ps 106:1)*

*Our Father . . .*

**Side 1:** Praise the Lord, all you nations; glorify him, all you peoples!

*(Ps 117:1)*

*Hail Mary . . .*

**Side 2:** For steadfast is his kindness toward us, and the fidelity of the Lord endures forever.

*(Ps 117:2)*

*Glory be . . .*

**V.** Let us pray:

**ALL:** Most high, all-powerful, all good, Lord! All praise is yours, all glory, all honor and all blessing. To you, alone, most high, do they belong. . . . Praise and bless my Lord, and give him thanks, and serve him with great humility.

(St. Francis, *Canticle of Brother Sun*)

\* \* \*

### Evening Prayer

**V.** In the name of the Father, and of the Son, and of the Holy Spirit.

**R. Amen.**

**Leader:** I will extol you, O my God and king, and I will bless your name forever and ever.

*(Ps 145:1)*

*Our Father . . .*

**Side 1:** Every day I will bless you, and I will praise your name forever and ever.

*(Ps 145:2)*

*Hail Mary . . .*

**Side 2:** Great is the Lord and highly to be praised; his greatness is unsearchable.

*(Ps 145:3)*

*Glory be . . .*

**Leader:** Praise the Lord, O my soul: I will praise the Lord all my life; I will sing praise to my God while I live.

*(Ps 146:1-2)*

*Our Father . . .*

**Side 1:** **Praise the Lord, for he is good, sing praise to our God, for he is gracious; it is fitting to praise him.**

*(Ps 147:1)*

*Hail Mary . . .*

**Side 2:** **Sing to the Lord with thanksgiving; sing praise with the harp to our God.**
*(Ps 147:7)*

*Glory be . . .*

**Leader:** Praise the Lord from the heavens, praise him in the heights.

*(Ps 148:1)*

*Our Father . . .*

**Side 1:** **Praise him, all you his angels; praise him, all you his hosts.**

*(Ps 148:2)*

*Hail Mary . . .*

**Side 2:** **Praise him, sun and moon; praise him, all you shining stars.**

*(Ps 148:3)*

*Glory be . . .*

**Leader:** Praise him, you highest heavens, and you waters above the heavens.

*(Ps 148:4)*

*Our Father . . .*

**Side 1:** **Let them praise the name of the Lord, for he commanded and they were created.**

*(Ps 148:5)*

*Hail Mary . . .*

**Side 2:** **Praise the name of the Lord, for his name alone is exalted; his majesty is above heaven and earth and he has lifted up the horn of his people.**

*(Ps 148:13-14)*

*Glory be . . .*

**Leader:** Praise the Lord in his sanctuary, praise him in the firmament of his strength.

*(Ps 150:1)*

*Our Father . . .*

**Side 1:** **Praise him for his mighty deeds, praise**

142

**him for his sovereign majesty.**

*(Ps 150:2)*

*Hail Mary . . .*

**Side 2:** **Praise him with the blast of the trumpet, praise him with lyre and harp.**

*(Ps 150:3)*

*Glory be . . .*

**Leader:** Praise him with timbrel and dance, praise him with strings and pipe.

*(Ps 150:4)*

*Our Father . . .*

**Side 1:** **Praise him with sounding cymbals, praise him with clanging cymbals.**

*(Ps 105:5)*

*Hail Mary . . .*

**Side 2:** **Let everything that has breath praise the Lord! Alleluia!**

*(Ps 150:6)*

*Glory be . . .*

**V.** Let us pray:

**ALL:** **All-powerful, all holy, most high and supreme God, sovereign good, all good, every good, you who alone are good, it is to you we must give all**

**praise, all glory, all thanks, all honor,
all blessing; to you we must refer all
good always. Amen.**

(St. Francis, Prayer, *The Praises before the Office*)

### THE OFFICE FOR A
### CHANGE OF HEART

*(This Office is particularly appropriate
for the Lenten Season.)*

**Morning Prayer**

**V.** In the name of the Father, and of the Son,
and of the Holy Spirit.

**R. Amen.**

**Leader:** Happy is he whose fault is taken away,
whose sin is covered.

*(Ps 32:1)*

*Our Father . . .*

**Side 1:** **Happy is the man to whom the Lord
imputes not guilt, in whose spirit there
is no guile.**

*(Ps 32:2)*

*Hail Mary . . .*

144

**Side 2:** Be glad in the Lord and rejoice, you just; exult, all you upright of heart.

*(Ps 32:11)*

*Glory be . . .*

**Leader:** As long as I would not speak, my bones wasted away with my groaning all the day.

*(Ps 32:3)*

*Our Father . . .*

**Side 1:** For day and night your hand was heavy upon me; my strength was dried up as by the heat of summer.

*(Ps 32:4)*

*Hail Mary . . .*

**Side 2:** Then I acknowledged my sin to you, my guilt I covered not; I said, "I confess my faults to the Lord," and you took away the guilt of my sin.

*(Ps 32:5)*

*Glory be . . .*

**Leader:** O Lord, all my desire is before you; from you my groaning is not hid.

*(Ps 38:10)*

*Our Father . . .*

**Side 1:** My heart throbs; my strength forsakes me; the very light of my eyes has failed me.

*(Ps 38:11)*

*Hail Mary . . .*

**Side 2:** Because for you, O Lord, I wait; you, O Lord my God, will answer.

*(Ps 38:16)*

*Glory be . . .*

**Leader:** Indeed, I acknowledge my guilt; I grieve over my sin.

*(Ps 38:19)*

*Our Father . . .*

**Side 1:** Forsake me not, O Lord; my God, be not far from me!

*(Ps 38:22)*

*Hail Mary . . .*

**Side 2:** Make haste to help me, O Lord my salvation!

*(Ps 38:23)*

*Glory be . . .*

**Leader:** Have mercy on me, O God, in your goodness; in the greatness of your compassion wipe out my offense.

*(Ps 51:3)*

*Our Father . . .*

**Side 1:** **Thoroughly wash me from my guilt and of my sin cleanse me.**

(Ps 51:4)

*Hail Mary . . .*

**Side 2:** **For I acknowledge my offense, and my sin is before me always.**

(Ps 51:5)

*Glory be . . .*

**Leader:** "Against you only have I sinned, and done what is evil in your sight"—That you may be justified in your sentence, vindicated when you condemn.

(Ps 51:6)

*Our Father . . .*

**Side 1:** **Indeed in guilt I was born, and in sin my mother conceived me.**

(Ps 51:7)

*Hail Mary . . .*

**Side 2:** **Behold, you are pleased with sincerity of heart, and in my inmost being you teach me wisdom.**

(Ps 51:8)

*Glory be . . .*

**V.** Let us pray:

**ALL:** **May the power of your love, O Lord, fiery and sweet as honey, wean my heart from all that is under heaven, so that I may die for love of your love, you who were so good as to die for love of my love.**

(St. Francis, Prayer, *Absorbeat*)

\* \* \*

## Evening Prayer

**V.** In the name of the Father, and of the Son, and of the Holy Spirit.

**R. Amen.**

**Leader:** Cleanse me of sin with hyssop, that I may be purified; wash me, and I shall be whiter than snow.

*(Ps 51:9)*

*Our Father . . .*

**Side 1:** **Let me hear the sounds of joy and gladness; the bones you have crushed shall rejoice.**

*(Ps 51:10)*

*Hail Mary . . .*

**Side 2:** Turn away your face from my sins, and blot out all my guilt.

*(Ps 51:11)*

*Glory be . . .*

**Leader:** A clean heart create for me, O God, and a steadfast spirit renew within me.

*(Ps 51:12)*

*Our Father . . .*

**Side 1:** Cast me not from your presence, and your holy spirit take not from me.

*(Ps 51:13)*

*Hail Mary . . .*

**Side 2:** Give me back the joy of your salvation, and a willing spirit sustain in me.

*(Ps 51:14)*

*Glory be . . .*

**Leader:** I will teach transgressors your ways, and sinners shall return to you. Free me from blood guilt, O God, my saving God; then my tongue shall revel in your justice.

*(Ps 51:15-16)*

*Our Father . . .*

**Side 1:** O Lord, open my lips, and my mouth shall proclaim your praise.

*(Ps 51:17)*

*Hail Mary . . .*

**Side 2:** For you are not pleased with sacrifices; should I offer a holocaust, you would not accept it. My sacrifice, O God, is a contrite spirit; a heart contrite and humbled, O God, you will not spurn.

*(Ps 51:18-19)*

*Glory be . . .*

**Leader:** Out of the depths I cry to you, O Lord; Lord, hear my voice.

*(Ps 130:1)*

*Our Father . . .*

**Side 1:** Let your ears be attentive to my voice in supplication.

*(Ps 130:2)*

*Hail Mary . . .*

**Side 2:** If you, O Lord, mark iniquities, Lord, who can stand?

*(Ps 130:3)*

*Glory be . . .*

**Leader:** But with you is forgiveness, that you may be revered.

*(Ps 130:4)*

*Our Father . . .*

**Side 1:** I trust in the Lord; my soul trusts in his word.

*(Ps 130:5)*

*Hail Mary . . .*

**Side 2:** My soul waits for the Lord more than sentinels wait for the dawn.

*(Ps 130:6a)*

*Glory be . . .*

**Leader:** More than sentinels wait for the dawn, let Israel wait for the Lord.

*(Ps 130:6b-7a)*

*Our Father . . .*

**Side 1:** For with the Lord is kindness and with him is plenteous redemption.

*(Ps 130:7b)*

*Hail Mary . . .*

**Side 2:** And he will redeem Israel from all their iniquities.

*(Ps 130:8)*

*Glory be . . .*

**V.**

**ALL:** . . . As we forgive those who trespass against us: And if we do not forgive perfectly, Lord, make us forgive perfectly, so that we may really love our enemies for love of you, and pray fervently to you for them, returning no one evil for evil, anxious only to serve everybody in you.

(St. Francis, *The Paraphrase of the Our Father*)

## OFFICE PRAYED WITH ST. FRANCIS

### SUNDAY

*Dominant idea of the day's Office: glorifying God by serving him.*

#### Morning Prayer

**V.** In the name of the Father, and of the Son, and of the Holy Spirit.

**R. Amen.**

**V.** Almighty, most high, holy and sovereign God, holy and just Father, Master of heaven and earth, for your own sake we give you thanks . . .

*Our Father, Hail Mary, Glory be.*

**V.** Because by your will, through your only Son, and in the Holy Spirit you have created all things spiritual and bodily.

*Our Father, Hail Mary, Glory be.*

**V.** We give you thanks, because just as you created us through your Son, so did you in that true and holy love with which you have loved us, have your Son be born of the glorious and ever Blessed Virgin, most holy Mary . . .

*Our Father, Hail Mary, Glory be.*

**V.** And it was your will to ransom us from our captivity with his cross and his blood.

*(First Rule of the Friars, c. 23)*

*Our Father, Hail Mary, Glory be.*

**V.** Almighty, most holy, high and sovereign God, the greatest good, the universal good, all that is good, you alone are good: may we render you all praise, all glory, all acknowledgment, all honor, and all blessing, and may we always refer to you whatever is good.

(The Praises before the Office)

*Our Father, Hail Mary, Glory be.*

**V.** Most high, mighty and good Lord,
Yours is the praise, the glory, the honor, and all benediction.
To you alone, Most High, do they belong,
And no man is fit even to mention your name.

(Canticle of the Creatures)

*Our Father, Hail Mary, Glory be.*

Scripture Reading: *(optional)*
Matthew 10:7-13

Meditation (moment of quiet prayer)

**V.** Let us pray:
O God, who, to enable us to walk in the ways of your only begotten Son, deigned to give us blessed Francis as a guide and teacher: mercifully grant that we may deserve to share in the heavenly glory of him whose memory we celebrate. Through the same Christ our Lord.

**R. Amen.**

\*       \*       \*

## Evening Prayer

**V.** In the name of the Father, and of the Son, and of the Holy Spirit.

**R. Amen.**

**V.** Observe, O man, to what distinction the Lord has raised you in creating you and molding you according to the image of his beloved Son bodily and according to his likeness spiritually.

*(Fifth Admonition)*

*Our Father, Hail Mary, Glory be.*

**V.** All the creatures under heaven in their way serve, recognize and obey their Creator better than you do.

*(Fifth Admonition)*

*Our Father, Hail Mary, Glory be.*

**V.** What we can take credit for are our infirmities and that we carry the holy cross of our Lord Jesus Christ day by day.

*(Fifth Admonition)*

*Our Father, Hail Mary, Glory be.*

**V.** Let us have no desire, no intention, no pleasure or delight apart from our Creator, Redeemer and Savior.

*(First Rule of the Friars, c. 23)*

155

*Our Father, Hail Mary, Glory be.*

**V.** They are pure of heart who disregard what the world offers and seek what heaven offers, never ceasing to adore and contemplate the true and living Lord God with a clean heart and mind.

*(16th Admonition)*

*Our Father, Hail Mary, Glory be.*

**V.** O almighty, eternal, just and merciful God, have us poor wretches for your sake do what we know you want, and have us always want whatever is pleasing to you.

*(Letter to the General Chapter)*

*Our Father, Hail Mary, Glory be.*

Scripture Reading: *(optional)*
Phil. 4:4-9

Meditation *(moment of quiet prayer)*

**V.** Let us pray:
O God, who through the merits of our blessed Father Francis, enlarged your Church with a new offspring: grant that, imitating him, we may despise earthly things and ever rejoice in partaking of heavenly gifts. Through Christ our Lord.

**R. Amen.**

# MONDAY

*Dominant idea of the day's Office: glorifying God by means of charity toward our neighbor.*

## Morning Prayer

**V.** In the name of the Father, and of the Son, and of the Holy Spirit.

**R. Amen.**

**V.** You are the holy Lord God, who alone works marvels. You are powerful, you are full of majesty, you are the Most High. You are the King of all might, you holy Father, King of Heaven and earth. You are the Lord God, who is threefold and one, and all that is good.

*Our Father, Hail Mary, Glory be.*

**V.** You are what is good, all that is good, the supreme good, true and living Lord God. You are charity, love. You are wisdom . . .

*Our Father, Hail Mary, Glory be.*

**V.** You are humility. You are patience. You are assurance. You are restfulness. You are joy and gladness. You are justice and temperance . . .

*Our Father, Hail Mary, Glory be.*

**V.** You are all the wealth one can desire. You are beauty. You are gentleness. You are our protector. You are our guardian and defender. You are strength. You are refreshment . . .

*Our Father, Hail Mary, Glory be.*

**V.** You are our hope. You are our faith. You are our great sweetness. You are our eternal life, great and marvelous Lord, God of all might, merciful Savior.

*(Praises of God)*

*Our Father, Hail Mary, Glory be.*

**V.** Be praised, my Lord, for all your creatures,
In special for Sir Brother Sun,
Who brings the day, and you give light to us through him.
And beautiful is he, agleam with mighty splendor,
He brings us understanding of you, Most High.

*(Canticle of the Sun)*

*Our Father, Hail Mary, Glory be.*

Scripture Reading: *(optional)*
    Matthew 5:13-16
Meditation *(moment of quiet prayer)*

158

**V.** Let us pray:
We beseech you, O Lord, may heavenly grace enlarge your Church, which you have been pleased to enlighten with the glorious merits and example of your confessor Blessed Francis. Through Christ our Lord.

**R.** Amen.

\*　　\*　　\*

### Evening Prayer

**V.** In the name of the Father, and of the Son, and of the Holy Spirit.

**R.** Amen.

**V.** Let any person who is entrusted with the obedience of others and who is regarded as someone greater, become like someone lesser and like the servant of the rest of the brethren.

*(Letter to All the Faithful)*

*Our Father, Hail Mary, Glory be.*

**V.** Since I am the servant of all, I am obliged to serve them all and to communicate to them the fragrant words of my Lord.

*(Letter to All the Faithful)*

*Our Father, Hail Mary, Glory be.*

**V.** Blessed is the person who does not keep

anything back for himself in giving Caesar what is Caesar's and God what is God's.

*(11th Admonition)*

*Our Father, Hail Mary, Glory be.*

**V.** I entreat all my friars in the charity which is God . . . not to boast, nor yet to take inner pleasure or be interiorly elated over the good words or deeds or anything good which God says or does or brings about at times in them or through them.

*(First Rule of the Friars, c. 17)*

*Our Father, Hail Mary, Glory be.*

**V.** How happy and blest are they who love the Lord and do what the Lord himself says in the Gospel.

*(Letter to All the Faithful)*

*Our Father, Hail Mary, Glory be.*

**V.** Do not keep anything of yourselves back for yourselves, so that he may have you altogether as his who has given himself altogether for you.

*(Letter to General Chapter)*

*Our Father, Hail Mary, Glory be.*

Scripture Reading: *(optional)*
  I Cor 13:1-13

Meditation (*moment of quiet prayer*)

**V.** Let us pray:
O God, who resists the proud and gives grace to the humble: grant, we beseech you, at the intercession of our holy Father St. Francis, that we may not be puffed up with pride, but may become more pleasing to you through humility; so that, walking in his footsteps, we may obtain the gifts of your grace. Through Christ our Lord.

**R.** **Amen.**

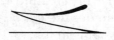

# TUESDAY

*Dominant idea of the day's Office: putting ourselves at God's disposal through poverty.*

### Morning Prayer

**V.** In the name of the Father, and of the Son, and of the Holy Spirit.

**R.** **Amen.**

**V.** You are worthy, O Lord, our God, to receive praise, glory and honor, and benediction...

*Our Father, Hail Mary, Glory be.*

**V.** Worthy is the Lamb who has been slain, to receive power and divinity and wisdom and might and honor and glory and benediction . . .

*Our Father, Hail Mary, Glory be.*

**V.** Let us bless the Father and the Son and the Holy Spirit. Let us praise him and extol him above all things, forever . . .

*Our Father, Hail Mary, Glory be.*

**V.** Him in his glory may heaven and earth praise, and every creature in heaven and on earth and under the earth, and no less the sea with what is in it . . .

*Our Father, Hail Mary, Glory be.*

**V.** Holy, holy, holy is the Lord God almighty, he who is and who was and who is to come . . .

*(The Praises before the Office)*

*Our Father, Hail Mary, Glory be.*

**V.** Be praised, my Lord, for Sister Moon and the Stars—
In the heavens you make them bright and fair and precious.
Be praised, my Lord, for Brother Wind,

And for the air, for cloudy, fair, and every kind of weather.
Through which you give your creatures sustenance.

*(Canticle of the Sun)*

*Our Father, Hail Mary, Glory be.*

Scripture Reading: *(optional)*
   Matthew 5:1-12

Meditation *(moment of quiet prayer)*

**V.** Let us pray:
   O God, who have given the soul of our blessed Father Francis the reward of everlasting bliss: mercifully grant that we, who devoutly commemorate his passing, may happily attain to the reward of the same bliss. Through Christ our Lord.

**R. Amen.**

\*    \*    \*

## Evening Prayer

**V.** In the name of the Father, and of the Son, and of the Holy Spirit.

**R. Amen.**

**V.** Such is the eminence of the most sublime poverty; it is that which has established

163

you as heirs and kings of the kingdom of
heaven.

*(Second Rule of the Friars, c. 6)*

*Our Father, Hail Mary, Glory be.*

**V.** Clinging to poverty in every way, for the
sake of our Lord Jesus Christ crave to have
nothing else under heaven at any time.

*(Second Rule, c. 6)*

*Our Father, Hail Mary, Glory be.*

**V.** He is truly poor in spirit, who hates himself
and loves those who slap his face.

*(14th Admonition)*

*Our Father, Hail Mary, Glory be.*

**V.** Holy Poverty confounds all grasping and
hoarding,
and the worries of this world as well.

*(Salute to the Virtues)*

*Our Father, Hail Mary, Glory be.*

**V.** The brethren should recall that our Lord
Jesus Christ, the Son of the almighty living
God, was poor and shelterless and lived on
alms—both he and the Blessed Virgin.

*(First Rule, c. 9)*

*Our Father, Hail Mary, Glory be.*

**V.** Let us be well on our guard against the guile and craftiness of Satan, who wants man not to keep his mind and heart set on God the Lord; as he prowls about, he aims at ravishing the heart of man with some sham recompense or advantage.

*(First Rule, c. 22)*

*Our Father, Hail Mary, Glory be.*

Scripture Reading: *(optional)*
  I Cor 1:18-25

Meditation *(moment of quiet prayer)*

**V.** Let us pray:
O God, who have caused the precious body of our blessed Father Francis to be brought forth from its hiding place to the light: grant, we beseech you, that we may escape the night of sin and direct our steps in the way of peace and justice. Through Christ our Lord.

**R.** Amen.

## WEDNESDAY

*Dominant idea of the day's Office: prayer as the safeguard of our Friendship with God.*

## Morning Prayer

**V.** In the name of the Father, and of the Son, and of the Holy Spirit.

**R. Amen.**

**V.** Our Father most holy, our Creator, our Redeemer and Savior, our Consoler . . .

*Our Father, Hail Mary, Glory be.*

**V.** Hallowed be your name: may we have a clearer knowledge of you, so that we may understand the breadth of your blessings, the length of your promises, the height of your majesty, and the depth of your judgments . . .

*Our Father, Hail Mary, Glory be.*

**V.** Your kingdom come: so that you may rule in us through grace and have us reach your kingdom . . .

*Our Father, Hail Mary, Glory be.*

**V.** Where there is the open sight of you, the perfect love of you, blissful association with you, everlasting enjoyment of you . . .

*Our Father, Hail Mary, Glory be.*

**V.** May your will be done on earth as it is in heaven: may we love you with all our heart

by always thinking of you, with all our soul
by always craving for you, with all our mind
by making you the aim of all our intentions
and seeking your honor in everything.

*(The Paraphrase of the Our Father)*

*Our Father, Hail Mary, Glory be.*

**V.** Be praised, my Lord, for Sister Water,
Most useful is she, and humble, and
precious and chaste.
Be praised, my Lord, for Brother Fire,
By which you light up the night;
And it is fair and gay, and hardy and strong.

*(Canticle of the Sun)*

*Our Father, Hail Mary, Glory be.*


Scripture Reading: *(optional)*
Matthew 11:25-30

Meditation *(moment of quiet prayer)*

**V.** Let us pray:
O God, who have glorified the body of our
blessed Father Francis with the stigmata of
your Son, and have wondrously elevated his
soul in heaven, graciously grant that we,
who keep his memory, may crucify our flesh
and its appetites here below, and thus become worthy to enter our heavenly home.

Through the same Christ our Lord.

**R. Amen.**

*     *     *

## Evening Prayer

**V.** In the name of the Father, and of the Son, and of the Holy Spirit.

**R. Amen.**

**V.** Where there is quiet and meditation, there is neither worry nor dissipation.

(27th Admonition)

*Our Father, Hail Mary, Glory be.*

**V.** Where there is fear of the Lord to guard the gateway,
there the Enemy can get no hold for an entry.

(27th Admonition)

*Our Father, Hail Mary, Glory be.*

**V.** Where there is patience and humility, there is neither anger nor loss of composure.

(27th Admonition)

*Our Father, Hail Mary, Glory be.*

**V.** Blessed is the servant that treasures up for heaven the favors God extends to him, and that has no desire to disclose them to people in the hope of a recompense, because the Most High himself will make his work known to whomever he wishes.

(28th Admonition)

*Our Father, Hail Mary, Glory be.*

**V.** The brethren should do their work with fidelity and devotion in such a way that they do not extinguish in themselves the spirit of holy prayer and recollection, to which all other things temporal should minister.

(Second Rule of the Friars, c. 5)

*Our Father, Hail Mary, Glory be.*

**V.** And since we are not fit to mention your name, we humbly entreat that our Lord Jesus Christ, your beloved Son, may render you thanks that please you, for everything; for he, through whom you have done so much for us, always suffices you for everything.

(First Rule of the Friars, c. 23)

*Our Father, Hail Mary, Glory be.*

Scripture Reading: *(optional)*
    Romans 8:26-30
Meditation *(moment of quiet prayer)*

**V.** Let us pray:

O God, who in many ways have disclosed the wonderful mysteries of the Cross in your most devoted confessor Blessed Francis: grant that your servants may always follow his example and obtain strength and virtue from constant meditation on the same Cross. Through Christ our Lord.

**R. Amen.**

## THURSDAY

*Dominant idea of the day's Office: love of God shown by devotion to the Holy Eucharist.*

### Morning Prayer

**V.** In the name of the Father, and of the Son, and of the Holy Spirit.

**R. Amen.**

**V.** Our Father most holy, our Creator, our Redeemer and Savior, and our Consoler, make us love you with all our strength, by spending all our forces and all the faculties of soul and body in the service of your love and on nothing else . . .

*Our Father, Hail Mary, Glory be.*

**V.** May we love our neighbors as ourselves, by getting them all as much as we can to love you . . .

*Our Father, Hail Mary, Glory be.*

**V.** Give us this day our daily bread—your beloved Son, our Lord Jesus Christ . . .

*Our Father, Hail Mary, Glory be.*

**V.** Give it to us today, so that we may remember, appreciate, and venerate the love he had for us, and all that he said and did and endured for us . . .

*Our Father, Hail Mary, Glory be.*

**V.** And forgive us our debts, in your unspeakable mercy and in virtue of the sufferings of your beloved Son, our Lord Jesus Christ.

*(The Paraphrase of the Our Father)*

*Our Father, Hail Mary, Glory be.*

**V.** Be praised, my Lord, for our sister Mother Earth,
Who sustains and guides us,
And brings forth fruits of many kinds, with varicolored flowers and grass.

*(Canticle of the Sun)*

*Our Father, Hail Mary, Glory be.*

Scripture Reading: *(optional)*
    John 13:1-5
Meditation *(moment of quiet prayer)*

**V.** Let us pray:

O God, who, to enable us to walk in the ways of your only begotten Son, deigned to give us Blessed Francis as a guide and teacher: mercifully grant that we may deserve to share in the heavenly glory of him whose memory we celebrate. Through the same Christ our Lord.

**R. Amen.**

\* \* \*

### Evening Prayer

**V.** In the name of the Father, and of the Son, and of the Holy Spirit.

**R. Amen.**

**V.** It is his Father's will that all of us be saved through him and should receive him with a clean heart and a chaste body.

*(Letter to All the Faithful)*

*Our Father, Hail Mary, Glory be.*

**V.** Let everybody halt in awe, let all the world quake, and let heaven exult, when Christ, the Son of the living God, is present on the altar.

*(Letter to the General Chapter)*

*Our Father, Hail Mary, Glory be.*

**V.** Bring all the reverence and all the respect you ever can to bear on the most holy body and blood of our Lord Jesus Christ, through whom whatever there is in heaven and on earth is appeased and reconciled to God almighty.

*(Letter to the General Chapter)*

*Our Fath‿ Hail Mary, Glory be.*

**V.** The Lord gave me such faith as regards churches that I prayed and said in simple fashion: We adore you, O Lord Jesus Christ, here and in every church all over the world, and bless you, because through your holy cross you have redeemed the world.

*(Testament)*

*Our Father, Hail Mary, Glory be.*

**V.** These most sacred mysteries I wish to see respected and venerated above all things, and kept in estimable places.

*(Testament)*

*Our Father, Hail Mary, Glory be.*

**V.** Please, O Lord, may the fiery, honeyed force of your love lap up my mind from everything under heaven: so that I may die for love of your love, who deigned to die for love of my love.

*(Authentic Prayers)*

*Our Father, Hail Mary, Glory be.*

Scripture Reading: *(optional)*
   I John 3:14-18
Meditation *(moment of quiet prayer)*

**V.** Let us pray:
   O God, who through the merits of our blessed Father Francis, enlarged your Church with a new offspring: grant that, imitating him, we may despise earthly things and ever rejoice in partaking of heavenly gifts. Through Christ our Lord.

**R. Amen.**

# FRIDAY

*Dominant idea of the day's Office:
renunciation of self after the example of Jesus.*

## Morning Prayer

**V.** In the name of the Father, and of the Son, and of the Holy Spirit.

174

**R. Amen.**

**V.** Clap your hands, all you nations, shout to God with a voice of rejoicing, for the Lord on high is terrible, the great king over all the earth . . .

*Our Father, Hail Mary, Glory be.*

**V.** For our most holy Father in heaven, our King, ages ago sent his beloved Son down from on high; and he has wrought salvation in the midst of the earth . . .

*Our Father, Hail Mary, Glory be.*

**V.** Let the heavens rejoice and the earth exult, let the sea be roused and the many things filling it, let the fields be glad with everything in them. Sing a new hymn to him. All the earth, sing to the Lord . . .

*Our Father, Hail Mary, Glory be.*

**V.** Bring to the Lord, O you countries of the gentiles, bring to the Lord glory and honor, bring the Lord glory for his name . . .

*Our Father, Hail Mary, Glory be.*

**V.** Bring your own person to carry his holy cross, and to follow his most holy commandments to the very end. Let all the earth be roused at his sight. Proclaim among the nations that the Lord is ruling.

*(Vespers Office of the Passion)*

*Our Father, Hail Mary, Glory be.*

**V.** Be praised, my Lord, for those who grant pardon for love of you,
And endure infirmity and tribulation.
Blessed are they who maintain themselves in peace,
For from you, Most High, they shall have their crown.

*(Canticle of the Sun)*

*Our Father, Hail Mary, Glory be.*

Scripture Reading: *(optional)*
Matthew 16:24-27

Meditation *(moment of quiet prayer)*

**V.** Let us pray:
We beseech you, O Lord, may heavenly grace enlarge your Church, which you have been pleased to enlighten with the glorious merits and example of your confessor Blessed Francis. Through Christ our Lord.

**R. Amen.**

\*　　\*　　\*

## Evening Prayer

**V.** In the name of the Father, and of the Son, and of the Holy Spirit.

**R. Amen.**

**V.** It was the Father's will that his blessed and glorious Son should offer himself as a sacrifice and victim on the altar of the cross by means of his own blood, leaving us an example to follow in his footsteps.

*(Letter to All the Faithful)*

*Our Father, Hail Mary, Glory be.*

**V.** It is for us to renounce ourselves and place our person under the yoke of service and holy obedience as each of us has promised the Lord.

*(Letter to All the Faithful)*

*Our Father, Hail Mary, Glory be.*

**V.** Blessed is the servant who always keeps the enemy (of his person) under control and guards himself prudently against him; for, let him do that, and no enemy visible or invisible can do him any harm.

*(Tenth Admonition)*

*Our Father, Hail Mary, Glory be.*

**V.** Let the time come when those who should

oblige the servant of God, do the contrary to him, and what degree of patience and humility he has then, that is the degree he has and no more.

*(13th Admonition)*

*Our Father, Hail Mary, Glory be.*

**V.** Holy Obedience confounds all selfishness of flesh and body, and keeps the body mortified to obey the spirit, and to obey one's fellow man.

*(Salute to the Virtues)*

*Our Father, Hail Mary, Glory be.*

**V.** The spirit of the Lord applies itself to humility and patience, to unaffected simplicity and true spiritual peace, and always craves to possess above all the fear of God, the Divine wisdom, and the Divine love of Father, Son, and Holy Spirit.

*(First Rule of the Friars, c. 17)*

*Our Father, Hail Mary, Glory be.*

Scripture Reading: *(optional)*
    Phil 3:8-14

Meditation *(moment of quiet prayer)*

**V.** Let us pray:
    O God, who resists the proud and gives

grace to the humble: grant, we beseech you, at the intercession of our holy Father St. Francis, that we may not be puffed up with pride, but may become more pleasing to you through humility; so that, walking in his footsteps, we may obtain the gifts of your grace. Through Christ our Lord.

**R. Amen.**

## SATURDAY

*Dominant idea of the day's Office:
devotion to Mary.*

### Morning Prayer

**V.** In the name of the Father, and of the Son, and of the Holy Spirit.

**R. Amen.**

**V.** Hear me, my brothers, children of the Lord, give ear to my words, incline the ear of your heart, and obey the voice of the Son of God . . .

*Our Father, Hail Mary, Glory be.*

**V.** Keep his commandments with all your heart, and comply with his counsels in a perfect spirit. Proclaim it that he is good, and exalt him in what you do . . .

*Our Father, Hail Mary, Glory be.*

**V.** For he has sent you out all over the world so that you might testify to his voice by what you say and do, and have everybody learn that there is no one almighty but he . . .

*Our Father, Hail Mary, Glory be.*

**V.** Persevere under discipline and holy obedience. What you have promised him, keep with a good and determined resolution . . .

*Our Father, Hail Mary, Glory be.*

**V.** The Lord God acts with you as with sons.

*(Letter to the General Chapter)*

*Our Father, Hail Mary, Glory be.*


**V.** Be praised, my Lord, for our brother the death of the body.
Which no man among the living can escape.
Unhappy they who will die in mortal sin.
Blessed those who shall be found in your most holy pleasure,
For the second death shall do no harm to them.

*(Canticle of the Sun)*

*Our Father, Hail Mary, Glory be.*

Scripture Reading: *(optional)*
    Mark 3:31-35
Meditation *(moment of quiet prayer)*


**V.** Let us pray:
    Hail, holy Lady,
        Most holy Queen,
        Mary, Mother of God,
        Ever Virgin;
    Chosen by the most holy Father in heaven,
        Consecrated by him,
        With his most holy beloved Son
        And the Holy Spirit, the Comforter.

    On you descended and in you still remains
        All the fulness of grace
        And every good.

    Hail, his Palace.
    Hail, his Tabernacle.
    Hail, his Robe.
    Hail, his Handmaid.
    Hail, his Mother.

    And Hail, all holy Virtues,
        Who, by the grace
        And inspiration of the Holy Spirit,
        Are poured into the hearts of the faithful
        So that, faithless no longer,

They may be made faithful servants of God
Through you.

(St. Francis, *Salutation of the Blessed Virgin*)

**R.** **Amen.**

\*     \*     \*

## Evening Prayer

**V.** In the name of the Father, and of the Son, and of the Holy Spirit.

**R.** **Amen.**

**V.** Hail, holy Lady, most holy Queen, Mother of God, Mary, a virgin forever, elected by the most holy Father in heaven and consecrated by him together with his most holy beloved Son and the Spirit the Paraclete.

(Salute to Mary)

*Our Father, Hail Mary, Glory be.*

**V.** O holy Virgin Mary, there is nobody like you born among women on earth. Daughter and handmaiden of the most high King, pray for us to your most holy and beloved Son, our Lord and Master.

(Office of the Passion)

*Our Father, Hail Mary, Glory be.*

**V.** The most high Father announced the

coming of this Word of the Father from heaven, through his archangel St. Gabriel, to the holy and glorious Virgin Mary, from whose womb he received the flesh of our human nature and frailty.

*(Letter to All the Faithful)*

*Our Father, Hail Mary, Glory be.*

**V.** If the blessed Virgin Mary is honored so much—and rightly so—because she bore Christ in her holy womb, how holy, just and worthy ought not anyone be who takes up Christ in his mouth and heart—Christ who is to live forever, Christ glorified, on whom the angels yearn to cast their glance?

*(Letter to the General Chapter)*

*Our Father, Hail Mary, Glory be.*

**V.** We are our Lord's mothers when we carry him about in our heart and person by means of love and a clean and sincere conscience, and we give birth to him by means of our holy actions, which should shine as an example to others.

*(Letter to All the Faithful)*

*Our Father, Hail Mary, Glory be.*

**V.** Almighty and eternal God, grant that we

may follow the footsteps of your Son, Jesus Christ, our Lord, and by means of your soul-saving grace come to you, the Most High, who in perfect trinity and simple unity live and reign and have all glory as the God of all might, world without end. Amen.

(Letter to the General Chapter)

*Our Father, Hail Mary, Glory be.*

Scripture Reading: *(optional)*
    I Cor 1:26-31

Meditation *(moment of quiet prayer)*

**V.** Let us pray:
Holy Virgin Mary, among all the women of the world there is none like you; you are the daughter and handmaid of the most high King and Father of heaven; you are the mother of our most holy Lord Jesus Christ; you are the spouse of the Holy Spirit. Pray for us, with Saint Michael the archangel and all the powers of heaven and all the saints, to your most holy and beloved Son, our Lord and Master.

**R. Amen.**

(St. Francis, *The Office of the Passion*)

# A MODEL WAKE SERVICE FOR SECULAR FRANCISCANS

## INTRODUCTION:

"Welcome, my Sister Death!" (II Cel., 217) With these words our Seraphic Father indicated his disposition toward that which causes fear and sorrow among much of the human family. The reality and tragedy of death cannot be ignored on the human level; and yet, as Christians we believe that death has "lost its sting" through the resurrection of the Lord Jesus. As Franciscans, we believe even more strongly that "it is in dying that we are born to eternal life." In view of this faith stance, death takes on an entirely new meaning. Thus, we celebrate the passing of a sister or brother to a new and more fruitful life in the company of

185

the saints. While we express our feelings of loss, we continue to hope and trust in the promises of Christ. Death teaches us to cling to the cross of the Lord with the knowledge that having "been conformed with him in his death, we will be conformed with him in his resurrection from death." (cf. Phil 3:10-11)

For our Father Francis, life was to search and strive for union with Christ through faith. Death was for him not a harsh reality, but the door through which he passed toward his ultimate goal—total union with the Father. What Francis sought through faith on earth, he achieved totally after death. The celebration of the death of a Franciscan shows forth the same faith as that which Francis possessed: our belief that death is the gateway to total union with God.

As the Franciscan Fraternity gathers to pray for its departed member, it seeks also to support one another in the faith which it shares. In this way the Fraternity expresses its sorrow at the parting which death has occasioned, and its joyful and confident hope of ultimate re-union with the deceased member and with the Lord. The Wake Service is a unique way for the Community to console one another at a time of loss and to honor the memory of one who now enjoys and shares in the triumph over death which has been won by the Lord.

The Wake Service takes the form of a Service of the Word. Members of the Fraternity gather in the funeral home at a convenient time, led by the president in prayer for the deceased. Other ministers include a reader and a leader of song. When the fraternity has gathered, the president begins:

**President:** (+) In the Name of the Lord. Amen. Grace and peace from God our Father and from the Lord Jesus Christ.

**ALL:** **May God be praised for his mercy to us, and may we experience his consolation now in our sorrow and be strengthened and enabled to share his love with all people.**

(If convenient, the president places a copy of the Rule of the Secular Franciscan Order in the casket with the body of the deceased saying:)

**President:** Our brother/sister N., was washed clean in baptism and nourished with the Body and Blood of the Lord in the Eucharist. As a Secular Franciscan, she/he was united more closely with the Lord and with us through the observance of our way of life. As she/he strove to follow this Rule of Life, may the Lord now take him/her to Himself and grant him/her a place among His saints in glory.

(The Fraternity then sings a suitable hymn, perhaps the "Peace Prayer" in one of its forms. Following the hymn, all are seated.)

**President:** As we contemplate the mystery of death and how it has affected our Fraternity in the passing of our brother/sister N., let us listen to the account of our Father Francis' passing to the Lord.

**Reader:** From the Major Life of St. Francis by Brother Bonaventure

As the moment of his death drew near, the saint had all the friars who were there called to his side; he spoke to them gently with fatherly affection, consoling them for his death and exhorting them to love God. He mentioned especially poverty and patient endurance and the necessity of holding to the faith of the holy Roman Church, and gave the Gospel preeminence over any other rule of life. The friars were grouped about him and he stretched out his arms over them in the form of a cross, because he loved that sign, and blessed all the friars, both present and absent, in the power and in the name of the Crucified. Then he added, "I bid you good-bye, all you my sons, in the fear of God. Remain in him always. There will be trials and temptations in the future, and it is well for those who persevere in the life they have undertaken. I am on my way to God, and I commend you all to his favor." When he had finished his inspiring admonition, he told them to bring a book of the Gospels and asked to have the passage of St. John read which begins, "Before the paschal feast began." Then, as best he could, he intoned the psalm, "Loud is my cry to the Lord, the prayer I utter for the Lord's mercy," and recited it all down to the last verse, "Too long have honest hearts waited to see you grant me redress."

At last, when all God's mysteries had been accomplished in him, his holy soul was freed from his body and assumed into the abyss of God's glory, and Francis fell asleep in God. One of the friars, a disciple of his, saw his soul being borne on a white cloud over many waters to heaven, under the appearance of a radiant star. It shone with the brightness of sublime sanctity, full of the abundance of divine wisdom and grace which had earned for him the right to enter the home of light and peace, where he rests with Christ forever. (Major Life, XIV, 5-6)

(A period of SILENT REFLECTION follows the reading and then the response, led by reader.)

**Reader:** All praise be yours, my Lord, through Sister Death,
From whose embrace no mortal can escape.

**ALL:** **All praise be yours, my Lord, through Sister Death,
From whose embrace no mortal can escape.**

**Reader:** Most high, all-powerful, all good, Lord!
All praise is yours, all glory, all honor
And all blessing.
To you, alone, Most High, do they belong.
No mortal lips are worthy
To pronounce your name.

**ALL:** **All praise be yours, my Lord, through Sister Death,**

**From whose embrace no mortal can escape.**

**Reader:** All praise be yours, my Lord, through all that you have made,
And first my lord Brother Sun,
Who brings the day; and light you give to us through him.
How beautiful is he, how radiant in all his splendor!
Of you, Most High, he bears the likeness.

**ALL:** **All praise be yours, my Lord, through Sister Death,**
**From whose embrace no mortal can escape.**

**Reader:** All praise be yours, my Lord, through Sister Moon and Stars;
In the heavens you have made them, bright
And precious and fair.
All praise be yours, my Lord, through Brothers Wind and Air,
And fair and stormy, all the weather's moods,
By which you cherish all that you have made.

**ALL:** **All praise be yours, my Lord, through Sister Death,**
**From whose embrace no mortal can escape.**

**Reader:** All praise be yours, my Lord, through Sister Water,
So useful, lowly, precious and pure.
All praise be yours, my Lord, through Brother Fire,
Through whom you brighten up the night.
How beautiful is he, how joyful! Full of power and strength.

**ALL:** **All praise be yours, my Lord, through Sister Death,**
**From whose embrace no mortal can escape.**

**Reader:** All praise be yours, my Lord, through Sister Earth, our mother,
Who feeds us in her sovereignty and produces
Various fruits with colored flowers and herbs.

**ALL:** **All praise be yours, my Lord, through Sister Death,**
**From whose embrace no mortal can escape.**

**Reader:** All praise be yours, my Lord, through those who grant pardon
For love of you; through those who endure
Sickness and trial.
Happy those who endure in peace,
By you, Most High, they will be crowned.

**ALL:** **All praise be yours, my Lord, through Sister Death,**
**From whose embrace no mortal can escape.**

**Reader:** Woe to those who die in mortal sin!
Happy those She finds doing your will!
The second death can do no harm to them.
Praise and bless my Lord, and give him thanks,
And serve him with great humility.

**ALL:** **All praise be yours, my Lord, through Sister Death,**
**From whose embrace no mortal can escape.**

### (Gospel Reading)

(A short period of quiet reflection follows the

response, and then a second reader—perhaps the leader of song—reads a Gospel passage, possibly Matthew 5:1-12. All stand for the Gospel reading.)

(After a period of silent reflection on the Gospel, or a short reflection given by the Fraternity president, the president introduces the General Intercessions:)

**President:** The Lord Jesus said: "I am the resurrection and the Life. Those who believe in me, even if they die, will live and every living person who puts faith in me will never suffer eternal death." Let us pray to him for our brother/sister N.

Lord Jesus, you raise those who sleep in death to life. Give N., our brother/sister Life Eternal.

**ALL:** **Lord, have mercy.**

**President:** You washed our brother/sister clean in the waters of baptism and sealed him/her with the seal of the Holy Spirit. Bring him/her to a place of light and refreshment in your Kingdom.

**ALL:** **Lord, have mercy.**

**President:** Our sister/brother was fed with your Body and Blood, may she/he find a place at table with you at the heavenly banquet.

**ALL:** **Lord, have mercy.**

**President:** Our brother/sister was united with us in the Franciscan Family. Grant him/her all that was promised by our Father Francis.

**ALL:** **Lord, have mercy.**

**President:** Remember us Lord, when you come into your Kingdom and teach us to pray:

**ALL:** **Our Father . . . . .**

**President:** Lord Jesus Christ, we trust in you, and hope in your glorious resurrection. Hear our prayers for our brother/sister N., whom you have called to yourself, and grant him/her eternal life.

We praise and glorify you who live in perfect Trinity and simple Unity with the Father and the Holy Spirit forever and ever.

**ALL:** **Amen.**

**President:** Before we take leave of our brother/sister for the last time, let us bless him/her with the Blessing of St. Francis.

(All raise their right hand toward the casket and together pray:)

**ALL:** May the Lord bless you and keep you.

May he show his face to you and be merciful to you.

May he turn his countenance to you and give you peace.

May the Lord bless you, brother/ sister N.

**President:** Our prayer for our brother/sister has ended. Let us go now, and until that time when the Lord shall gather us all into his Kingdom, let us live in his peace.

**ALL:** Thanks be to God.

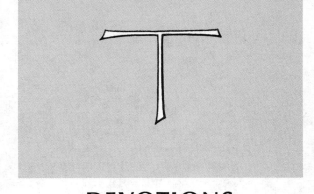

# DEVOTIONS

# PRAYERS BEFORE THE BLESSED SACRAMENT

## Act of Dedication of the Human Race to the Sacred Heart

Jesus, Redeemer of the human race, look down upon us. We are yours and yours we wish to be; but in order to be still more firmly united to you, today each one of us freely dedicates himself to your most Sacred Heart. There are many indeed who have never known you; many others have rejected your commandments and have disowned you. Be merciful to all of them, O kind Jesus, and draw them all to your holy Heart. Be king, O Lord, not only of the faithful who have never abandoned you, but also of the prodigal children who have left you; bring them back quickly to their Father's house lest they die of misery and hunger. Be king of those who have been deceived by erroneous ideas or have been separated by discord; bring them back to the harbor of truth and to the unity of faith so that soon there may be a single fold and a single shepherd. Bestow upon your Church, O Lord, security, liberty, and safety; give to all nations the tranquility of order; and grant that from one pole of the earth to the other there may ring out the cry: Praise to the divine Heart which brought forth our salvation; to it be glory and honor forever. Amen.

## For Help in Deciding
## One's State in Life

Give me the grace, merciful God, to desire earnestly and gladly whatever way of life is pleasing to you, to seek it prudently, to recognize it honestly, to follow it perfectly.

Arrange my way of life to the praise and glory of your name; and, whatever it is your will that I should do, give me the light to see it and grace duly to carry it out, for so it will be well with me.

### Prayer for Religious Vocations

O God, * who does not desire the death of

the sinner, * but rather that he be converted and live, * grant, we beseech you, * through the intercession of Blessed Mary ever Virgin * and of all the saints, * an increase of laborers for your Church, * who, cooperating with Christ, * may give themselves and generously spend themselves for the salvation of souls, * through the same Jesus Christ, your Son our Lord, * who lives and reigns with you in union with the Holy Spirit, * world without end. Amen.

*Three Hail Marys for vocations.*

## Prayer of St. Francis for Peace

Dear Jesus, make me an instrument of your peace. * Where there is hatred * let me sow love * where there is injury * pardon: * where there is doubt * faith: * where there is despair * hope: * where there is darkness * light: * and where there is sickness * joy.

O divine Master * grant that I may not so much seek to be consoled * as to console: * to be understood * as to understand: * to be loved * as to love: * for it is in giving that we receive: * it is in pardoning that we are pardoned: * and it is in dying * that we are born to eternal life. Amen.

## For Priests

O God, * whose ways all show mercy and truth, * continue your kindly work, * and by your goodness * give what is impossible to human frailty; * that they who minister at the heavenly mysteries * may in their faith be perfect, * and, in the purity of their souls, * be a light that will shine forth to all. Amen.

## Acts of Spiritual Communion

Jesus, my Savior and my God! I am not worthy to appear before you, * for I am a poor sinner; * yet I approach you with confidence, * for you have said, * "Come to me, all you that labor and are heavy-laden, * and I will refresh you." * You will not despise a contrite and humble heart. * I am truly sorry for my sins, * because by them I have offended you, * who are infinitely good. * Whatever may have been my foolish transgressions in the past, * I love you now above all things, * and with all my heart. * I desire, good Jesus, * to receive you in Holy Communion, * and since I cannot now receive you in the Blessed Sacrament, * I beseech you to come to me spiritually * and to refresh my soul with your sweetness.

Come, my Lord, * my God, and my all! Come

to me, * and let me never again be separated from you by sin. * Teach me your blessed ways; * help me with your grace to imitate your example; * to practice meekness, * humility, * charity, * and all the virtues of your Sacred Heart. * My divine Master, * my one desire is to do your will * and to love you more and more; * help me that I may be faithful to the end * in your service. * Bless me in life and in death, * that I may praise you forever in heaven. Amen.

## Prayer before Benediction

O most loving Jesus, who are about to bestow your benediction * upon all who are here assembled, * I humbly beg that it may impart to each one of us * the special graces of which we stand in need. * If your all-powerful hand bless us, * we shall be blessed indeed.

Bless then, O Lord, our bodies * that they may be strong and active only in your service. * Bless our souls * that they may become a perfect image of yourself. * Bless our minds * that they may realize the vanity of earthly riches, honors, and pleasures, * and esteem only virtue and the treasures of heaven. * Bless our wills * that they may submit in all things to your most holy will * and cooperate always with your divine grace. * Bless our hearts, * and purify them from all inordinate affections and worldly desires * that they may beat only for love of you.

Let your blessing, O Jesus, * go forth far and wide. * May it descend upon our dear parents, * relatives, * benefactors, * friends, * and upon all those who are especially devoted to you * in the Sacrament of your love. * Let it be felt by the poor, * the sick, * and the afflicted, * and by all those who cannot come hither to receive it. * Let the weak and tempted feel its power; * and let poor sinners, * especially those who are to die this day, * be aroused * to repentance and return to you.

Let your benediction, O Jesus, * cross the deserts and the seas * and animate the missionaries * toiling in the fields afar * for souls so dear to your most Sacred Heart. * Let it penetrate to the realms of Purgatory * and prove a soothing balm to the Holy Souls suffering there * and longing to be united with you.

O Jesus, * I beg your blessing for myself * and for all who are near and dear to me. * I beg it for all those for whom you wish me to pray *

and for those who have recommended themselves to my prayers. * May it accomplish in us
all that sublime purpose * for which, O Lord,
you so lovingly impart it. Amen.

## Tantum Ergo

### Benediction

*The Divine Praises*

Blessed be God.

Blessed be his Holy Name.

Blessed be Jesus Christ, true God and true
Man.

Blessed be the Name of Jesus.

Blessed be his most Sacred Heart.

Blessed be Jesus in the most Holy Sacrament
of the Altar.

Blessed be his most Precious Blood.

Blessed be the Holy Spirit, the Paraclete.

Blessed be the great Mother of God, Mary most
Holy.

Blessed be her holy and Immaculate Conception.

Blessed be her glorious Assumption.

Blessed be the name of Mary, virgin and
mother.

Blessed be St. Joseph, her most chaste spouse.

Blessed be God in his angels and in his saints.

# THE STATIONS OF THE CROSS

## Preparatory Prayer

Most merciful Jesus, in a contrite and penitent spirit * I bow down before your divine Majesty. * I adore you as my supreme Lord and Master; * I believe in you; * I hope in you; * I love you above all things. * I am heartily sorry for having offended you, my only and supreme God, * I firmly resolve to amend my life; * and although I am unworthy to obtain mercy, * yet the sight of your holy Cross * fills me with peace and consolation. * I will, therefore, meditate on your passion * and visit the stations * in company with your sorrowful Mother and my holy Guardian Angel * to promote your honor and to save my soul.*

O loving Jesus, * inflame my cold heart with your love * that I may perform this devotion as perfectly as possible * and that I may live and die in union with you. Amen.

# I
# JESUS IS SENTENCED TO DEATH
## Meditation

**P.** The most innocent Jesus is condemned to the ignominious death of the cross. In order to remain a friend of Caesar, Pilate delivers Jesus into the hands of his enemies. O fearful crime, to condemn innocence to death and to displease God in order to please man.

We adore you, O Christ, and praise you.

**C. Because by your holy Cross you have redeemed the world.**

## Prayer

**C. O innocent Jesus, \* I have sinned and I am guilty of eternal death. \* But you gladly accept the unjust sentence of death \* that I may live. \* For whom, then, shall I henceforth live, \* if not for you, my Lord. \* Should I desire to please man, \* I cannot be your servant. \* Let me, therefore, rather displease the whole world \* than not to please you, O Jesus. Amen.**

**Our Father. Hail Mary.**

**P.** Lord Jesus, crucified.

**C. Have mercy on us.**

# II
## JESUS TAKES HIS CROSS

### Meditation

**P.** When our divine Redeemer beheld the Cross, he most willingly stretched out his bleeding arms, embraced it lovingly, kissed it tenderly, placed it on his bruised shoulders, and although quite exhausted, carried it joyfully.

We adore you, O Christ, and praise you.

**C. Because by your holy Cross you have redeemed the world.**

### Prayer

**C. O my Jesus, * I cannot be your friend and follower, * if I refuse to carry the Cross. * O beloved Cross, * I embrace you, I kiss you, I joyfully accept you from the hand of my God. * Far be it from me to glory in anything * save in the Cross of my Lord and Redeemer. * By it the world shall be crucified to me and I to the world * that I may be yours forever. Amen.**

**Our Father. Hail Mary.**

**P.** Lord Jesus, crucified.

**C. Have mercy on us.**

# III
## JESUS FALLS THE FIRST TIME

### Meditation

**P.** Our dear Savior carrying the Cross was so weakened by its heavy weight as to fall exhausted to the ground. The cross was light and sweet, but our sins made it heavy and oppressive to him.

We adore you, O Christ, and praise you.

**C.** Because by your holy Cross you have redeemed the world.

### Prayer

**C.** Beloved Jesus, * you carried the heavy weight of my sins. * Shall I not bear in union with you the light burden of my sufferings * and accept the sweet yoke of your commandments? * Your yoke is sweet and your burden is light. * I willingly take up my cross and follow you. Amen.

Our Father. Hail Mary.

**P.** Lord Jesus, crucified.

**C.** Have mercy on us.

# IV
## JESUS MEETS HIS BLESSED MOTHER

### Meditation

**P.** How painful it must have been for Mary to behold her beloved Son laden with the Cross, covered with wounds and blood, and driven through the streets by savage executioners. What unspeakable pangs her most tender heart must have felt. How earnestly did she desire to die instead of Jesus or at least with him!

We adore you, O Christ, and praise you.

**C.** Because by your holy Cross you have redeemed the world.

### Prayer

**C.** O Jesus, O Mary! * I am the cause of the pains that pierced your hearts. * Would that my heart could experience some of your sufferings. * O Mother, * let me partake in your sufferings and those of your Son * that thereby I may obtain the grace of a happy death. Amen.

**Our Father. Hail Mary.**

**P.** Lord Jesus, crucified.

**C.** Have mercy on us.

# V
## SIMON HELPS JESUS TO CARRY HIS CROSS

### Meditation

**P.** Simon of Cyrene was compelled to help the exhausted Savior carry his Cross. How pleased Jesus would have been had Simon offered his services. But remember, Simon was not invited by Christ as you are. He says: "Take your cross and follow me." But you complain and carry it reluctantly.

We adore you, O Christ, and praise you.

**C.** **Because by your holy Cross you have redeemed the world.**

### Prayer

**C.** **O Jesus, * whoever does not take up his cross and follow you * is not worthy of you. * Behold, I cheerfully join you on the way of the Cross. * I desire to carry my cross patiently until death * that I may become worthy of you. Amen.**

**Our Father. Hail Mary.**

**P.** Lord Jesus, crucified.

**C.** **Have mercy on us.**

# VI
## VERONICA WIPES THE FACE OF JESUS

### Meditation

**P.** Moved by compassion, Veronica presents her veil to Jesus to wipe his blood-stained face. He imprints on it his holy countenance and returns it to her as a recompense. Shall Christ reward you in like manner? Then must you also do him a service. This you do every time you perform a work of mercy, for he says: "What you have done to the least of my brethren you have done to me."
We adore you, O Christ, and praise you.

**C. Because by your holy Cross you have redeemed the world.**

### Prayer

**C. Dearest Jesus, * what return shall I make you for all your benefits? Behold, I consecrate myself entirely to your service. * I give you my whole heart; * stamp thereon your holy image * that I may never forget you. Amen.**

**Our Father. Hail Mary.**

**P.** Lord Jesus, crucified.

**C. Have mercy on us.**

# VII
## JESUS FALLS THE SECOND TIME

### Meditation

**P.** Borne down by the weight of the Cross, Jesus again falls to the ground. But the cruel executioners will not permit him to rest a moment. With blows and curses they urge him onward. How cruelly Jesus is treated and trampled under foot. Remember compassionate soul, that your sins caused Jesus this painful fall.

We adore you, O Christ, and praise you.

**C. Because by your holy Cross you have redeemed the world.**

### Prayer

**C. Have mercy on me, O Jesus, * and do not permit me to relapse into sin. * From this very moment I will earnestly strive never to sin again. * Do you, O Jesus, * strengthen me with your grace, * that I may faithfully carry out my resolution. Amen.**

**Our Father. Hail Mary.**

**P.** Lord Jesus, crucified.

**C. Have mercy on us.**

# VIII
## JESUS SPEAKS TO THE HOLY WOMEN
### Meditation

**P.** Moved by compassion, these devoted women weep over the suffering Savior. But he turns to them saying: "Weep not for me, but for yourselves and your children; weep for your sins and those of your children, for they are the cause of my passion." You, too, must weep over your sins; for there is nothing more pleasing to our Lord and more useful than the tears shed through contrition for your sins.

We adore you, O Christ, and praise you.

**C.** **Because by your holy Cross you have redeemed the world.**

### Prayer

**C.** **O Jesus, * give to my eyes a torrent of tears * that I may day and night weep for my sins. I beseech you by your bitter and bloody tears to move my heart * that from my eyes tears may flow abundantly, * and that I may weep until death over your passion and over my sins. Amen.**

**Our Father. Hail Mary.**

**P.** Lord Jesus, crucified.

**C.** **Have mercy on us.**

# IX
## JESUS FALLS THE THIRD TIME

### Meditation

**P.** Arriving exhausted at the foot of Calvary, Jesus falls for the third time to the ground. By these repeated falls all the wounds of his tender body were reopened. How enormous must be my sins that caused Jesus these painful falls! Had he not taken my sins upon himself, they would have plunged me into the abyss of hell.

We adore you, O Christ, and praise you.

**C.** **Because by your holy Cross you have redeemed the world.**

### Prayer

**C.** **Most merciful Jesus, * I give you a thousand thanks for not permitting me to die in my sins * and to fall into the abyss of hell * as I have so often deserved. * Enkindle in me an earnest desire to amend my life. * Let me never again fall into sin, * but grant me the grace of final perseverance. Amen.**

**Our Father. Hail Mary.**

**P.** Lord Jesus, crucified.

**C.** **Have mercy on us.**

# X
# JESUS IS STRIPPED OF HIS GARMENTS
## Meditation

**P.** Having arrived on Calvary, Jesus was cruelly deprived of his garments. This caused him the greatest pain because the garments adhered to his mangled body, and with them parts of his skin were torn away. Jesus is deprived even of his garments that he may die possessed of nothing. How happy shall I die after laying aside my evil habits and tendencies!
We adore you, O Christ, and praise you.

**C.** Because by your holy Cross you have redeemed the world.

## Prayer

**C.** Let me, O Jesus, amend my life; * and let it be renewed according to your will and desire. * However painful this may be to me, I will not spare myself. * With the help of your grace I will refrain from all vain and sinful pleasures * that I may live and die in your holy grace. Amen.
Our Father. Hail Mary

**P.** Lord Jesus, crucified.

**C.** Have mercy on us.

# XI
## JESUS IS NAILED TO THE CROSS

### Meditation

**P.** Stripped of his garments, Jesus is violently thrown upon the Cross. His hands and feet are most cruelly nailed thereto. Jesus remains silent because it so pleases his heavenly Father. He suffers patiently because he suffers for you. How do you act in sufferings and trials? How fretful and impatient are you! How prone to complain! We adore you, O Christ, and praise you.

**C.** **Because by your holy Cross you have redeemed the world.**

### Prayer

**C.** **O Jesus, * meek and patient Lamb, * I deplore my impatience. * Crucify, O Lord, my flesh with all its evil desires and vices. * Punish and afflict me in this life, but spare me in the next. * I resign myself entirely to your holy Will. * May it be done in all things. Amen.**

**Our Father. Hail Mary.**

**P.** Lord Jesus, crucified.

**C.** **Have mercy on us.**

# XII
## JESUS DIES ON THE CROSS
### Meditation

**P.** Behold Jesus crucified. Behold his wounds received for love of you. His whole appearance betokens love. His head is bent to kiss you. His arms are extended to embrace you. His heart is open to receive you. Jesus dies on the Cross that you may be preserved from eternal death.

We adore you, O Christ, and praise you.

**C.** **Because by your holy Cross you have redeemed the world.**

### Prayer

**C.** **Most amiable Jesus, \* would I could die for love of you. \* I will endeavor to die to the world and its vanities \* when I behold you hanging on the Cross \* covered with wounds, \* crowned with thorns. \* Merciful Jesus \* receive me into your wounded heart \* that I may despise all perishable things and live for you alone. Amen.**

**Our Father. Hail Mary.**

**P.** Lord Jesus, crucified.

**C.** **Have mercy on us.**

# XIII
## JESUS IS TAKEN FROM THE CROSS

## Meditation

**P.** Jesus did not descend from the Cross, but he remained on it till his death. When taken down, he rested on the bosom of his beloved Mother as he had so often done in life. Persevere in your good resolutions, and do not flee from the Cross, for he who perseveres till the end shall be saved.

We adore you, O Christ, and praise you.

**C.** **Because by your holy Cross, you have redeemed the world.**

## Prayer

**C.** **O Lord Jesus crucified, * I most earnestly entreat you to aid me in doing good, * and not to let me be separated from your Cross; * for on it I desire to live and to die. * Create in me a clean heart * that I may receive worthily your most sacred Body in Holy Communion, * and that you may remain in me and I in you for all eternity. Amen.**

**Our Father. Hail Mary.**

**P.** Lord Jesus, crucified.

**C.** **Have mercy on us.**

# XIV
## JESUS IS LAID IN THE TOMB

### Meditation

**P.** The body of Jesus is laid in a stranger's tomb. He who in life had not whereon to lay his head would have no grave of his own after death. You whose heart is yet attached to this world, despise it that you may not perish with it.

We adore you, O Christ, and praise you.

**C.** **Because by your holy Cross, you have redeemed the world.**

### Prayer

**C.** **O Jesus, * you have set me apart from the world. * What then shall I seek in it? * You have created me for heaven; * what then shall I desire upon earth? * Depart from me, deceitful world, with your vanities. * Henceforth I will walk the way of the Cross, traced out for me by my Redeemer, * and journey onward to my heavenly fatherland, * where my home and my rest will be forever. Amen. Our Father. Hail Mary.**

**P.** Lord Jesus, crucified.

**C.** **Have mercy on us.**

## Conclusion

C. Lord Jesus, I thank you, * for all the graces you have granted me during these stations. * I offer this devotion to promote your greater honor, * to obtain the pardon of my sins, * to console and help the souls in purgatory, * particularly those for whom I intended to gain these indulgences. * I beseech you, O Jesus, * do not permit the infinite value of your precious Blood, * of your bitter passion and death * to be lost in my regard; * do not permit that my soul, so dearly bought by you, perish forever; * but conduct it in the way that leads to you, * to eternal joy and glory. Amen.

# MAY DEVOTIONS

### Prayer to the Blessed Virgin

HOLY MARY, Mother of God, * we are assembled here today * to show our love and veneration to you. We rejoice at the dignity and glory which the Lord has bestowed upon you; * we praise and bless him for having given us a Mother * adorned with so pure and tender a heart.

We consecrate to you, * O holy Virgin and dearest Mother, * this entire month, and especially this day. We choose you as our Mother, patroness, and advocate with Jesus, your beloved Son, * now and forever.

We consecrate to you our soul and body; * to you we recommend all our wishes and desires, * our prayers and studies, * our crosses and trials, * our whole life, and especially the end thereof. Show yourself a mother to us.

We recommend to you the whole Catholic Church, * our sovereign pontiff, * our bishop, * the priests and religious, * our parents, superiors, benefactors, relatives, friends and enemies, * and the souls of the faithful departed.

O Blessed Virgin Mary, * graciously hear our prayers and receive our petitions, * which we unite with those of all the faithful on earth * and of the angels and saints in heaven. Amen.

*Rosary*
*Hymn*
*Litany of the B.V.M.* (p. 255)

## Memorare

Remember, O most gracious Virgin Mary * that never was it known * that any one who had recourse to your protection, * implored your help, * and sought your mediation, * was left unaided. * Inspired with this confidence, * I fly unto you, * O Virgin of virgins, my Mother. To you I come; * before you I stand, sinful and sorrowful. * O Mother of the Word Incarnate, * despise not my petitions, * but in your mercy hear and answer me. Amen.

*Benediction*

# THE MYSTERIES OF THE ROSARY
## The Joyful Mysteries

### 1. The Annunciation.

In this mystery we consider how the Archangel Gabriel announced to the Blessed Virgin Mary, that she was to conceive and bear a Son, our Lord Jesus Christ.

### 2. The Visitation.

In this mystery we consider that when Mary learned that Elizabeth had conceived, she went to visit her and remained with her three months.

### 3. The Nativity.

In this mystery we consider that the Blessed Virgin brought forth the Savior of the world in the stable of Bethlehem.

### 4. The Presentation.

In this mystery we consider how the Blessed Virgin, on the day of her purification, presented Christ our Lord in the temple.

### 5. The Finding of Christ in the Temple.

In this mystery we consider how the

Blessed Virgin lost her divine Son, and found him after three days amidst the doctors in the temple.

## The Sorrowful Mysteries

### 1. The Agony in the Garden.

In this mystery we consider how our dear Lord suffered the agony of death in the garden of Gethsemane.

### 2. The Scourging.

In this mystery we consider how the Savior was most cruelly scourged at the pillar.

### 3. The Crowning with Thorns.

In this mystery we consider how our Lord Jesus Christ was crowned with sharp thorns.

### 4. The Carrying of the Cross.

In this mystery we consider how Christ carried the heavy Cross up Mount Calvary.

### 5. The Crucifixion.

In this mystery we consider how our divine Savior was crucified and died on the Cross.

# The Glorious Mysteries

**1. The Resurrection.**

    In this mystery we consider how Jesus Christ our Lord arose from the dead on the third day, glorious and triumphant.

**2. The Ascension.**

    In this mystery we consider how the Savior, forty days after his resurrection, triumphantly ascended into heaven.

**3. The Sending of the Holy Spirit.**

    In this mystery we consider how our divine Savior on Pentecost sent the Holy Spirit, in the form of tongues of fire, upon his apostles.

**4. The Assumption.**

    In this mystery we consider how our divine Savior took his blessed Mother up into heaven with soul and body.

**5. The Coronation.**

    In this mystery we consider how our divine Savior crowned his blessed Mother as Queen of heaven and earth.

*Hymn*
*Litany of the B.V.M.* (p. 255)

# NOVENAS

## NOVENA IN HONOR OF THE IMMACULATE CONCEPTION

### Prayer of St. Alphonsus

O most holy and immaculate Virgin, * my Mother, * you are the Mother of my Lord, * the Queen of the world, * the Advocate, Hope, and Refuge of sinners! I now come to you. I venerate you, great Queen, * and give you thanks * for the many favors you have bestowed on me in the past; * most of all * I thank you for having saved me from hell, * which I had so often deserved. * I love you, * Lady most worthy of all love; * and, by the love which I bear you, * I promise ever in the future * to serve you and to do all in my power * to win others to your love. * In you I put all my trust, * all my hope of salvation. * Receive me as your servant * and cover me with the mantle of your protection, * you who are the Mother of mercy.

* And since you have so much power with God, * deliver me from all temptations; * or at least obtain for me * the grace ever to overcome them. * From you I ask a true love of Jesus Christ * and the grace of a happy death. * O my Mother, * by your love for God * I beseech you to be at all times my helper, * but above all at the last moment of my life. * Leave me not * until you see me safe in heaven, * there for endless ages to bless you and sing your praises. Amen.

Three Our Fathers, etc., to obtain the grace of holy purity.

**V.** In your conception, O Virgin, you were immaculate.

**R.** Pray for us to the Father, whose Son was born of you.

Let us pray:

O God, who, by the Immaculate Conception of the Blessed Virgin Mary, prepared a worthy habitation for your Son, we beseech you that as, by the foresight of his death, you exempted her from all stain, so we, purified by her intercession, may come to you through the same Jesus Christ, our Lord, who lives and reigns with you and the Holy Spirit world without end. Amen.

# CHRISTMAS DEVOTION

## *Hymn*

**V.** INCLINE unto my aid, O God.

**R.** O Lord, make haste to help me.

**V.** Glory be to the Father and to the Son and to the Holy Spirit.

**R.** As it was in the beginning, is now, and ever shall be world without end. Amen.

**C.** Jesus, Sweetest Child, who, * coming down from the bosom of the Father * for our salvation, * did not disdain the womb of the Virgin, * where * conceived by the Holy Spirit, * you, * the Word Incarnate, * took upon yourself the form of a servant, * have mercy on us.

**V.** Have mercy on us, Child Jesus.

**R.** Have mercy on us.

Hail Mary.

**C.** Jesus, Sweetest Child, born in Bethlehem of the Virgin Mary, * wrapped in swaddling clothes, * laid in a manger, * heralded by angels, * visited by shepherds, * have mercy on us.

**V.** Have mercy on us, Child Jesus,

**R.** Have mercy on us.

Hail Mary.

**C.** Jesus, Sweetest Child, made known to the Magi by a star, * adored on Mary's bosom, * honored with the mystical gifts of gold, * frankincense, * and myrrh, * have mercy on us.

**V.** Have mercy on us, Child Jesus,

**R.** Have mercy on us.
   Hail Mary.

**C.** Jesus, Sweetest Child, whom Herod sought to slay, * whom St. Joseph carried with Mary into Egypt, * who was saved by flight from a cruel death, * and glorified by the praises of the Holy Innocents, * have mercy on us.

**V.** Have mercy on us, Child Jesus,

**R.** Have mercy on us.
   Hail Mary.

*Hymn*

**C.** Jesus, Sweetest Child, who with Mary most holy, * and the patriarch St. Joseph, * dwelt in Egypt until the death of Herod, * have mercy on us.

**V.** Have mercy on us, Child Jesus,

**R.** Have mercy on us.

**C.** Jesus, Sweetest Child, brought to Jerusalem when twelve years old, * sought by your parents with much sorrow, * and after three days, * found to their great joy among the doctors, * have mercy on us.

**V.** Have mercy on us, Child Jesus,

**R.** Have mercy on us.

**V.** The Word was made flesh.

**R.** And dwelt among us.

Let us pray:

**P.** Almighty and eternal God, * Lord of heaven and earth, * who reveal yourself to little ones, * grant us, we beseech you, * properly to honor the holy mysteries of your Son, * the Child Jesus, * and to follow him humbly in our lives, * so that we may come to the eternal kingdom * promised by you to little ones; * through the same Jesus Christ, our Lord, * your Son, * who lives and reigns with you * in the unity of the Holy Spirit, * world without end. Amen.

## CHAIR OF UNITY OCTAVE

Our Father. Hail Mary. Glory be to the Father (*three times*).

**Ant.** That they all may be one, as you, Father, in me and I in you; that they also may be one in us; that the world may believe that you have sent me.

**V.** I say unto you, that you are Peter.

**R.** And upon this rock I will build my Church.

Let us pray:

O Lord Jesus Christ, who did say unto your Apostles: "Peace I leave with you. My peace I give unto you"; regard not our sins, but the faith of your Church, and grant unto her that peace and unity which are agreeable to your will, who live and reign God forever and ever. Amen.

## Octave Intentions

Jan. 18—The union of all Christians in the one true faith and in the Church.

Jan. 19—The return of separated Eastern Christians to communion with the Holy See.

Jan. 20—The reconciliation of Anglicans with the Holy See.

Jan. 21—The reconciliation of European Protestants with the Holy See.

Jan. 22—That American Christians become one in union with the Chair of Peter.

Jan. 23—The restoration of lapsed Catholics to the sacramental life of the Church.

Jan. 24—That the Jewish people come into their inheritance in Jesus Christ.

Jan. 25—The missionary extension of Christ's
kingdom throughout the world.

## NOVENA TO ST. JOSEPH

TO YOU, O blessed Joseph * we have recourse in our affliction. * By that charity which
bound you to the Immaculate Virgin, Mother
of God, * and by the fatherly love with which
you embraced the Child Jesus, * look down, we
beseech you, * with gracious eye on the
precious inheritance * which Jesus Christ pur-
chased with his blood, * and help us in our
necessities by your power and aid, * Protect,
O most watchful guardian of the Holy Family, *
the elect children of Jesus Christ; * ward off
from us, O most loving father, * all blight of
error and corruption; * and, even as of old you
rescued the Child Jesus from the greatest peril
of his life, * so now defend God's Holy Church
* from the snares of the enemy * and from all
adversity. * Shield also each one of us by your
constant protection, * so that, supported by
your example and your aid, * we may live a
holy life, * die a happy death, * and attain everlasting happiness in heaven. Amen.

Remember, O most pure St. Joseph, my beloved patron, * that never has it been heard *

that anyone invoked your patronage and sought your aid without being comforted. * Inspired by this confidence, * I come to you and fervently commend myself to you. * O despise not my petition, * dear foster-father of our Redeemer, * but accept it graciously. Amen.

*Litany of St. Joseph* (p. 258)


# NOVENA OF TUESDAYS TO ST. ANTHONY

## Traditional Prayer

O GLORIOUS St. Anthony, * safe refuge of the afflicted and distressed, * who by a miraculous revelation * have directed all those who seek aid * to come to your altar, * with the promise * that whoever visits it for nine consecutive Tuesdays, * and there piously invokes you, * will feel the power of your intercession, * I, a poor sinner, * encouraged by this promise, * come to you, O powerful Saint, * and with a firm hope I implore your aid, * your protection, * your counsel, and your blessing. * Obtain for me, I beseech you, * my request in this necessity (think of your request). * But if it should be opposed to the will of God * and the welfare of my soul, * obtain for me such other graces *

as shall be conducive to my salvation. *
Through Christ our Lord. Amen.

  Our Father, Hail Mary. Glory be to the Father.

**V.** Pray for us, O blessed Anthony,

**R.** That we may be made worthy of the
promises of Christ.

Let us pray:

**P.** Almighty and eternal God, who glorified
your faithful confessor Anthony with the
perpetual gift of working miracles,
graciously grant that what we confidently
seek through his merits, we may surely
receive through his intercession. Through
Christ our Lord. Amen.

**To the Infant Jesus in the Arms of St. Anthony**

**C.** O Jesus, my Savior! * Who vouchsafed to
appear to St. Anthony in the form of an
infant, * I implore you, * through the love
you bore to this saint when he dwelt on
earth, * and which you now bear to him in
heaven, * graciously hear my prayer * and
assist me in my necessities, * who live and
reign world without end. Amen.

## Aspirations to St. Anthony

**V.** St. Anthony, our patron and our advocate.

**R.** Grant us what we ask of you.

**V.** St. Anthony, powerful in word and work.

**R.** Grant us what we ask of you.

**V.** St. Anthony, attentive to those who invoke you.

**R.** Grant us what we ask of you.

**V.** St. Anthony, glory of the Church and honor of the Franciscan Order,

**R.** Grant us what we ask of you.

**V.** St. Anthony, whom the Infant Jesus so much loved and honored,

**R.** Grant us what we ask of you.

**V.** Pray for us, Blessed Anthony.

**R.** That we may be made worthy of the promises of Christ.

Let us pray:

O God, let the votive commemoration of your confessor and doctor Blessed Anthony be a source of joy to your Church, that she may always be fortified with spiritual assistance and may deserve to possess eternal joy. Through Christ, our Lord. Amen.

## NOVENA IN HONOR
## OF THE HOLY SPIRIT

COME, Holy Spirit, Creator blest,
And in our souls take up your rest,
Come with your grace and heav'nly aid,
To fill the hearts which you have made.

Come, O Spirit of Wisdom, dispose my heart, so that I may learn to value and love the good things of heaven, and prefer them to all earthly delights. Show me, moreover, the way whereby I may obtain and possess them forever.

Hail Mary, etc.

Come, O Spirit of Understanding, enlighten my mind, that I may apprehend and embrace all the mysteries of salvation, and deserve to behold the Light eternal in your light, and to attain the full knowledge of you and the Father and the Son.

Hail Mary, etc.

Come, O Spirit of Counsel, be with me in all the affairs of this passing life, incline my soul unto good, withhold it from evil, and guide me through the straight path of your commandments to the desired goal of everlasting salvation.

Hail Mary, etc.

Come, O Spirit of Fortitude, give strength to

my heart in every trouble and mishap; grant me power against the baneful efforts of my enemies, lest, being overcome, I be parted from you, O God, the sovereign Good.

Hail Mary, etc.

Come, O Spirit of Knowledge, grant that I may understand the emptiness of worldly goods. Teach me to despise them, and to use them for your glory alone, and to prize your everlasting treasures beyond all earthly things.

Hail Mary, etc.

Come, O Spirit of Godliness, stir up my heart to true fervor and to a holy love of the Lord my God, that I may ever seek him in all my devotions, and may find him in true love.

Hail Mary, etc.

Come, O Spirit of the Fear of the Lord, make my flesh tremble with fear of you, that I may set the Lord before me always, and may carefully avoid whatever may displease the most pure eyes of your divine Majesty.

Hail Mary, etc.

**V.** Come, Holy Spirit, fill the hearts of your faithful.
**R.** And kindle in them the fire of your love.

Let us pray:

O God who, by the light of the Holy Spirit, has taught the hearts of your faithful, grant that we may be truly wise in the same Spirit and ever rejoice in his consolation. Through Christ our Lord. Amen.

*Hymn*

Great Paraclete! to you we cry,
O highest gift of God Most High!
O Fount of life! O Fire of Love!
And sweet anointing from above!

## NOVENA TO THE MOST SACRED HEART OF JESUS

**V.** O GOD, come to my assistance.

**R.** O Lord, make haste to help me.

**V.** Glory be to the Father, etc.

**R.** As it was in the beginning, etc.

**C.** Most loving Jesus, when I ponder over your most sacred Heart, * all tenderness and sweetness for sinners, * then does my heart rejoice, * and I am filled with the hope of a kind welcome. * But my sins! * How many and how great they are! * With Peter I bewail them, * because they are an offense to you, my sovereign God. * Oh, grant me

239

pardon for them all. * I pray your Sacred Heart that I may rather die than offend you again, * and may live only to love you.

**V.** O Heart of Jesus, I implore,

**R.** That I may love you more and more.

**C.** My Jesus, I bless, your most humble Heart; and I give thanks unto you, who in making it my model * urge me with the strongest pleadings to imitate it, * and also, at the cost of so many humiliations, * vouchsafe yourself * to point out and smooth the way to follow you. * Fool that I am, * how have I wandered far away from you! * Pardon me my Jesus. * Take away from me all hateful pride and ambition, * that with a lowly heart I may follow you, my Jesus, * amidst humiliations, * and so gain peace and salvation. * Strengthen me, and I will ever bless your Sacred Heart.

**V.** O Heart of Jesus, I implore,

**R.** That I may love you more and more.

**C.** My Jesus, I marvel at your most patient Heart, and I give you thanks * for all the wondrous examples of unwearied patience * which you have left us. * It grieves me that these examples * still have to reproach me for my excessive delicacy, * shrinking from every little pain. * Pour, then, into my heart, O dear Jesus, * fervent and constant love of suffering and the Cross, * of mortification and penance, * that, following you to Calvary, * I may with you attain the joys of paradise.

V. O Heart of Jesus, I implore,
R. That I may love you more and more.

C. Dear Jesus, beside your most gentle Heart, I set my own, * and shudder to see how unlike mine is to yours. * How I fret and grieve * when a hint, * a look, * or a word thwarts me. * Pardon my violence * and for the future give me grace * to imitate in every contradiction your unalterable meekness, * that so I may enjoy an everlasting holy peace.

V. O Heart of Jesus, I implore,
R. That I may love you more and more.

C. Let us sing praise to Jesus—for his most generous Heart, * the conqueror of death and hell, * for well it merits every praise. * Still more confounded am I, * looking upon my coward heart, * which dreads even a rough word or injurious taunt. * But it shall be so with me no more. * My Jesus. * I pray you for such strength that, * fighting and conquering self on earth, * I may one day rejoice triumphantly with you in heaven.

**V.** O Heart of Jesus, I implore,

**R.** That I may love you more and more.

**C.** Now let us turn to Mary, * dedicating ourselves yet more and more to her; * and trusting in her Mother's heart, we say to her: * By all the virtue of your heart * obtain for me, * great Mother of God, our Mother Mary, * a true and enduring devotion to the Sacred Heart of Jesus your Son, * that, bound up in every thought and affection in union with his heart, * I may fulfill each duty of my state, * serving Jesus ever more with readiness of heart, * and especially this day.

**V.** Heart of Jesus, burning with love for us.

Let us pray:

**C.** Lord, we beseech you, * let your Holy Spirit kindle in our hearts that fire of charity * which our Lord Jesus Christ, your Son, * sent forth from his inmost Heart upon this earth, * and willed that it should burn exceedingly. * Who lives and reigns with you, * in the unity of the same Holy Spirit, * God forever and ever. Amen.

*Litany of the Sacred Heart* (p. 250)

# NOVENA IN HONOR OF ST. FRANCIS

I GREET and venerate you, Holy Father, St. Francis, who lived in the greatest poverty * and tormented your innocent body with every rigor. * with kind violence tear me away from the world and its deceits, * and turn all my affections to God. * Intercede for me * that I may overcome my evil inclinations * and henceforth lead a pure and holy life.

I greet and venerate you, * Holy Father, St. Francis, * upon whose body our divine Savior * impressed the marks of his sacred wounds. Obtain for me an ardent devotion to the passion of Christ, * that I may cheerfully bear the Cross * and produce worthy fruits of penance.

I greet and venerate you, * Holy Father, St. Francis, * who died of longing for God. * I invite you with Jesus and Mary * to assist me at the hour of my death. * Be then to me a father and protector and intercede for me, * that I may die in the grace of God and merit to dwell in heaven, * where you now enjoy everlasting glory. Amen.

C. Holy Father, amiable and most beloved St. Francis, I beseech you by the holy wounds of our Lord Jesus Christ, * which were imprinted on your body, * assist me to govern the five senses of my body, * according to the will and pleasure of almighty God. * Intercede for me * and obtain for me contrition and devotion, * faith, hope, and charity, * patience, * purity of body and soul, * together with the grace of persevering in the service of the Lord; * so that after this life * I may merit to come to you * and with you enjoy eternal happiness, * which I hope through your intercession * to obtain from Christ our Lord. Amen.

*Hymn*

C. O seraphic Father, St. Francis, I venerate you, * the living image of Christ crucified. * Born like him in a stable, * you condemned a world which rejected you; * poor like him * you esteemed no possessions * but those which are eternal; * meek and humble like him, * you counted confusion and humiliation a joy; inflamed with an ardent charity, * you burned to increase his glory; * your love transformed your whole life into one long martyrdom, * and made you strive by severe penances * to satisfy the ardor of your desires, * until at last it impressed on your

244

body * the wounds it had long before engraved deeply in your heart, * and made you
a living crucifix, * preaching sweetly to men
the sufferings and love of Jesus.

Obtain for me, * O holy Father, * that I too
may banish from my heart the spirit of the
world; * that I may esteem poverty and humiliation above wealth and honors; * that I may
mortify my passions * and advance daily in the
knowledge and love of God, * until at last, *
detached from myself, * from the world, * and
from all creatures, * I may live for God alone, *
and like you, may say with my whole heart: *
My God and my all, * my inheritance, and my
joy * in time and in eternity. Amen.

# LITANIES

## LITANY OF THE HOLY NAME OF JESUS

Lord, have mercy on us,
  *Christ, have mercy on us.*
Lord, have mercy on us,
Jesus, hear us,
  *Jesus, graciously hear us.*
God, the Father of heaven, *
God, the Son, Redeemer of the world,
God, the Holy Spirit,
Holy Trinity, one God,
Jesus, Son of the living God,
Jesus, splendor of the Father,
Jesus, brightness of eternal light,
Jesus, King of glory,
Jesus, sun of justice,
Jesus, Son of the Virgin Mary,
Jesus, most amiable,
Jesus, most admirable,

---

*Have mercy on us.*

Jesus, mighty God,
Jesus, Father of the world to come,
Jesus, angel of the great counsel,
Jesus, most powerful,
Jesus, most patient,
Jesus, most obedient,
Jesus, meek and humble of heart,
Jesus, lover of chastity,
Jesus, lover of us,
Jesus, God of peace,
Jesus, author of life,
Jesus, model of virtues,
Jesus, zealous of souls,
Jesus, our God,
Jesus, our refuge,
Jesus, Father of the poor,
Jesus, treasure of the faithful,
Jesus, good shepherd,
Jesus, true light,
Jesus, eternal wisdom,
Jesus, infinite goodness,
Jesus, our way and our life,
Jesus, joy of angels,
Jesus, king of patriarchs,
Jesus, master of the apostles,
Jesus, teacher of the evangelists,
Jesus, strength of martyrs,

Jesus, light of confessors,
Jesus, purity of virgins,
Jesus, crown of all saints,
Be merciful,
   *Spare us, O Jesus.*
Be merciful,
   *Graciously hear us, O Jesus.*
From all evil, **
From all sin,
From your wrath,
From the snares of the devil,
From the spirit of uncleanness,
From eternal death,
From the neglect of your inspirations,
Through your nativity,
Through the mystery of your holy incarnation,
Through your childhood,
Through your most divine life,
Through your labors,
Through your agony and passion,
Through your cross and abandonment,
Through your sufferings,
Through your death and burial,
Through your resurrection,
Through your ascension,

--------

*\*\*Jesus deliver us.*

Through your institution of the most holy
Eucharist,
Through your joys,
Through your glory,
Lamb of God, who takes away the sins of the
world,
*Spare us, O Jesus.*
Lamb of God, who takes away the sins of the
world,
*Graciously hear us, O Jesus.*
Lamb of God, who takes away the sins of the
world,
*Have mercy on us, O Jesus.*
Jesus, hear us.
*Jesus, graciously hear us.*

Let us pray:

O Lord Jesus Christ, who has said: Ask and
you shall receive; seek and you shall find;
knock and it shall be opened unto you; we
beseech you, grant unto us who beg of you the
gift of your most divine charity, that we may
love you with our whole heart, in word and
deed, and never desist from your praise.

Grant us, O Lord, continual fear and love of
your Holy Name; for you never abandon the
care of those whom you solidly establish in

your love. Through our Lord, Jesus Christ, your
Son, who lives and reigns with you, in the unity
of the Holy Spirit, world without end. Amen.

## LITANY OF THE SACRED HEART

Lord, have mercy on us,
*Christ, have mercy on us.*
Lord, have mercy on us,
Christ, hear us.
*Christ, graciously hear us.*
God, the Father of Heaven,*
God, the Son, Redeemer of the world,
God, the Holy Spirit,
Holy Trinity, one God,
Heart of Jesus, Son of the Eternal Father,
Heart of Jesus, formed by the Holy Spirit in the
   womb of the Virgin Mother,
Heart of Jesus, substantially united to the
   Word of God,
Heart of Jesus, of Infinite Majesty,
Heart of Jesus, Sacred Temple of God,
Heart of Jesus, Tabernacle of the Most High,
Heart of Jesus, House of God and Gate of
   Heaven,

---

*Have mercy on us.*

Heart of Jesus, burning furnace of charity,
Heart of Jesus, abode of justice and love,
Heart of Jesus, full of goodness and love,
Heart of Jesus, abyss of all virtues,
Heart of Jesus, most worthy of all praise,
Heart of Jesus, King and Center of all hearts,
Heart of Jesus, in whom are all the treasures of wisdom and knowledge,
Heart of Jesus, in whom dwells the fulness of Divinity,
Heart of Jesus, in whom the Father was well pleased,
Heart of Jesus, of whose fulness we have all received,
Heart of Jesus, desire of the everlasting hills,
Heart of Jesus, patient and most merciful,
Heart of Jesus, enriching all who invoke you,
Heart of Jesus, fountain of life and holiness,
Heart of Jesus, propitiation for our sins,
Heart of Jesus, loaded down with opprobrium,
Heart of Jesus, bruised for our offenses,
Heart of Jesus, obedient unto death,
Heart of Jesus, pierced with a lance,
Heart of Jesus, source of all consolation,
Heart of Jesus, our life and resurrection,
Heart of Jesus, our peace and reconciliation,
Heart of Jesus, victim of sin,

Heart of Jesus, salvation of those who trust in you,

Heart of Jesus, hope of those who die in you,

Heart of Jesus, delight of all the saints,

Lamb of God, who take away the sins of the world,

*Spare us, O Lord.*

Lamb of God, who take away the sins of the world,

*Graciously hear us, O Lord.*

Lamb of God, who take away the sins of the world,

*Have mercy on us.*

**V.** Jesus, meek and humble of heart,

**R.** Make our hearts like unto yours.

Let us pray:

O almighty and eternal God, look upon the Heart of your dearly beloved Son, and upon the praise and satisfaction he offers you in behalf of sinners, and, being appeased, grant pardon to those who seek your mercy, in the name of the same Jesus Christ, your Son, who lives and reigns with you, in the unity of the Holy Spirit, world without end. Amen.

# LITANY OF THE MOST PRECIOUS BLOOD

Lord, have mercy on us.
*Christ, have mercy on us.*
Lord, Have mercy on us.
Christ, Hear us.
*Christ, graciously hear us.*

God, the Father of Heaven,*
God, the Son, Redeemer of the world,
God, the Holy Spirit,
Holy Trinity, One God,
Blood of Christ, only-begotten Son of the Eternal Father, **
Blood of Christ, Incarnate Word of God,
Blood of Christ, of the New and Eternal Testament,
Blood of Christ, falling upon the earth in the Agony,
Blood of Christ, shed profusely in the Scourging,
Blood of Christ, flowing forth in the Crowning with Thorns,
Blood of Christ, poured out on the Cross,
Blood of Christ, price of our salvation,
Blood of Christ, without which there is no forgiveness,

---

*Have mercy on us.*
**Save us.*

Blood of Christ, Eucharistic drink and refreshment of souls,
Blood of Christ, stream of mercy,
Blood of Christ, victor over demons,
Blood of Christ, courage of martyrs,
Blood of Christ, strength of confessors,
Blood of Christ, bringing forth virgins,
Blood of Christ, help of those in peril,
Blood of Christ, relief of the burdened,
Blood of Christ, solace in sorrow,
Blood of Christ, hope of the penitent,
Blood of Christ, consolation of the dying,
Blood of Christ, peace and tenderness of hearts,
Blood of Christ, pledge of eternal life,
Blood of Christ, freeing souls from purgatory,
Blood of Christ, most worthy of all glory and honor,
Lamb of God, who take away the sins of the world,
  *Spare us, O Lord.*
Lamb of God, who take away the sins of the world,
  *Graciously hear us, O Lord.*
Lamb of God, who take away the sins of the world,
  *Have mercy on us.*

**V.** You have redeemed us, O Lord, in your Blood,

**R.** And made us, for our God, a Kingdom.

Let us pray:

Almighty and Eternal God, you have appointed your only-begotten Son the Redeemer of the world, and willed to be appeased by his Blood. Grant, we beg of you, that we may worthily adore this price of our salvation, and through its power be safe-guarded from the evils of this present life, so that we may rejoice in its fruits forever in heaven. Through the same Christ our Lord. Amen.

## LITANY OF THE BLESSED VIRGIN

Lord, have mercy on us,
*Christ, have mercy on us.*
Lord, have mercy on us,
Christ, hear us.
*Christ, graciously hear us.*
God, the Father of Heaven,*
God the Son, Redeemer of the world,
God, the Holy Spirit,
Holy Trinity, one God,

---

*Have mercy on us,*

Holy Mary,**
Holy Mother of God,
Holy Virgin of virgins,
Mother of Christ,
Mother of divine grace,
Mother most pure,
Mother most chaste,
Mother inviolate,
Mother undefiled,
Mother most amiable,
Mother most admirable,
Mother of good counsel,
Mother of our Creator,
Mother of our Redeemer,
Virgin most prudent,
Virgin most venerable,
Virgin most renowned,
Virgin most powerful,
Virgin most merciful,
Virgin most faithful,
Mirror of justice,
Seat of wisdom,
Cause of our joy,
Spiritual vessel,
Vessel of honor,
Singular vessel of devotion,

---

**Pray for us.*

Mystical rose,
Tower of David,
Tower of ivory,
House of gold,
Ark of the covenant,
Gate of heaven,
Morning star,
Health of the sick,
Refuge of sinners,
Comforter of the afflicted,
Help of Christians,
Queen of angels,
Queen of patriarchs,
Queen of prophets,
Queen of apostles,
Queen of confessors,
Queen of martyrs,
Queen of virgins,
Queen of all saints,
Queen, conceived without original sin,
Queen, assumed into Heaven,
Queen of the most holy Rosary,
Queen of peace,
Queen of the Franciscan Order,
Lamb of God, who take away the sins of the
    world,
    *Spare us, O Lord.*

Lamb of God, who take away the sins of the world,
*Graciously hear us, O Lord.*
Lamb of God, who take away the sins of the world,
*Have mercy on us.*

**V.** Pray for us, O Holy Mother of God.
**R.** That we may be made worthy of the promises of Christ.

Let us pray:

Grant, we beseech you, O Lord God, that we your servants may enjoy perpetual health of mind and body, and through the intercession of the blessed Mary ever Virgin, may be delivered from present sorrow and obtain eternal joy. Through Christ our Lord. Amen.

## LITANY OF ST. JOSEPH

Lord, have mercy on us,
*Christ, have mercy on us.*
Lord, have mercy on us,
Christ, hear us.
*Christ, graciously hear us.*
God, the Father of heaven,*
God, the Son, Redeemer of the world,

---

*Have mercy on us.*

God, the Holy Spirit,
Holy Trinity, one God,
St. Joseph,
Holy Mary, **
Illustrious descendant of David,
Light of patriarchs,
Spouse of the Mother of God,
Chaste guardian of the Virgin,
Foster-father of the Son of God,
Zealous defender of Christ,
Head of the holy Family,
Joseph, most just,
Joseph, most chaste,
Joseph, most prudent,
Joseph, most valiant,
Joseph, most obedient,
Joseph, most faithful,
Mirror of patience,
Lover of poverty,
Model of workmen,
Ornament of the domestic life,
Guardian of virgins,
Safeguard of families,
Consolation of the poor,
Hope of the sick,
Patron of the dying,

---

**Pray for us.*

Terror of the demons,
Protector of holy Church,
Lamb of God, who take away the sins of the
world,
*Spare us, O Lord.*
Lamb of God, who take away the sins of the
world,
*Graciously hear us, O Lord.*
Lamb of God, who take away the sins of the
world,
*Have mercy on us.*

**V.** He made him lord of his household,
**R.** And ruler of all his possessions.

Let us pray:

O God, who in your ineffable Providence
deigned to choose blessed Joseph to be the
spouse of your most holy Mother, grant, we
beseech you, that we may deserve to have him
for our intercessor in heaven whom on earth
we venerate as our holy protector. Who live
and reign world without end. Amen.


## LITANY OF ALL SAINTS

Lord have mercy,
*Lord, have mercy*

Christ, have mercy,
  *Christ, have mercy*
Lord, have mercy,
  *Lord, have mercy;* or:
God, our Father in heaven,
  *Have mercy on us*
God the Son, our Redeemer,
  *Have mercy on us*
God the Holy Spirit
  *Have mercy on us.*
Holy Trinity, one God
  *Have mercy on us.*
Holy Mary,*
Mother of God,
Most honored of all virgins,
Michael, Gabriel, and Raphael,
Angels of God.
Abraham, Moses and Elijah,
St. John the Baptist,
St. Joseph,
Holy Patriarchs and Prophets.
St. Peter, and St. Paul,
St. Andrew,
St. John, and St. James,
St. Thomas,
St. Matthew,

---

*Pray for us.*

All holy Apostles,
St. Luke,
St. Mark,
St. Barnabas,
St. Mary Magdalene,
All Disciples of the Lord.
St. Stephen,
St. Ignatius,
St. Polycarp,
St. Justin,
St. Lawrence,
St. Cyprian,
St. Boniface,
St. Stanislaus,
St. Thomas Becket,
St. John Fisher and St. Thomas More,
St. Paul Miki,
St. Isaac Jogues and St. John de Brebeuf,
St. Peter Chanel,
All holy Martyrs for Christ.
St. Leo and St. Gregory,
St. Ambrose,
St. Jerome,
St. Augustine,
St. Athanasius,
St. Basil and St. Gregory,
St. John Chrysostom,

St. Martin,
St. Patrick,
St. Cyril and St. Methodius,
St. Charles Borromeo,
St. Francis de Sales,
St. Pius,
St. Anthony,
St. Benedict,
St. Bernard,
St. Francis and St. Dominic,
St. Thomas Aquinas,
St. Ignatius Loyola,
St. Francis Xavier,
St. Vincent de Paul,
St. John Vianney,
St. John Bosco,
St. Catherine,
St. Theresa,
St. Rose,
St. Louis,
St. Monica,
St. Elizabeth,
All holy men and women.
Lord be merciful,
*Lord, save your people*
From all evil,*

---

*Lord, save your people*

From every sin,
From the snares of the devil,
From anger and hatred,
From every evil intention,
From everlasting death,
By your coming as man,
By your birth,
By your baptism and fasting,
By your sufferings and cross,
By your death and burial,
By your rising to new life,
By your return in glory to the Father,
By your gift of the Holy Spirit,
By your coming again in glory; or:
Christ, Son of the living God,
　*Have mercy on us*
You came into this world,**
You suffered for us on the cross,
You died to save us,
You lay in the tomb,
You rose from the dead,
You returned in glory to the Father,
You sent the Holy Spirit upon your Apostles,
You are seated at the right hand of the Father,
You will come again to judge the living and the
　dead.

─────────────

**Have mercy on us*

Lord, be merciful to us,
*Lord, hear our prayer*
Give us true repentance,*
Strengthen us in your service,
Reward with eternal life all who do good to us,
Bless the fruits of the earth and of man's labor; or:
Lord, show us your kindness,
Raise our thoughts and desires to you,
Save us from final damnation,
Save our friends and all who have helped us,
Grant eternal rest to all who have died in the faith,
Spare us from disease, hunger, and war,
Bring all peoples together in trust and peace.
Guide and protect your holy Church,
Keep the pope and all the clergy in faithful service to your Church.
Bring all Christians together in unity,
Lead all men to the light of the gospel.
Christ, hear us,
*Christ, hear us*
Lord Jesus, hear our prayer,
Lord Jesus, hear our prayer; or:
Lamb of God, you take away the sins of the world,

---

*Lord, hear our prayer

*Have mercy on us*

Lamb of God, you take away the sins of the world,
*Have mercy on us*

Lamb of God, you take away the sins of the world,
*Have mercy on us.*

Let us pray:

God of love, our strength and protection, hear the prayers of your Church. Grant that when we come to you in faith, our prayers may be answered through Christ our Lord;

or:

Lord God, you know our weakness. In your mercy grant that the example of your Saints may bring us back to love and serve you through Christ our Lord.

## A FRANCISCAN LITANY OF ALL SAINTS

Lord, have mercy! *Lord, have mercy!*
Christ, have mercy! *Christ, have mercy!*
Lord, have mercy! *Lord, have mercy!*
God, the Father, *have mercy on us!*
God, the Son, *have mercy on us!*
God, the Holy Spirit, *have mercy on us!*
Holy Trinity, one God, *have mercy on us!*

*     *     *

Holy Mary, the Immaculate Conception, Queen of the Franciscan Order,
  *pray for us!*
Holy Father Francis, (1226 - Oct. 4)*
  *pray for us!*

       \*       \*       \*

All you holy martyrs of the Franciscan Order,
  *pray for us!*
Saints Berard, Accursius, Adjutus, Otto, and Peter, Protomartyrs (1220 - Jan. 16)
  *pray for us!*
Saints Daniel, Angelo, Domnus, Hugolinus, Leo, Nicholas, and Samuel, Martyrs of Africa, (1227 - Oct. 10)
  *pray for us!*
Saints Nicholas Tavelic, Deodat of Aquitaine, Peter of Narbonne, and Stephen of Cuneo, Martyrs of the Holy Land, (1391 - Nov. 14)
  *pray for us!*
Saint Thomas More, Martyr of England, (1535 - June 22)
  *pray for us!*

---

*The year indicates date of death. The month and day is that of the solemnity, feast, or memorial, and usually it is the day of death. This litany lists only the canonized Franciscan saints and all of them, a total of 125.

Saints Nicholas Pick, Anthony Hornaer, Anthony of Weert, Cornelius, Francis, Godfrey, Jerome, Nicasius, Peter, Theodoric, Willehad, Martyrs of Holland, (1572 - July 9)
*pray for us!*

Saints Peter Baptist Blasquez, Martin de Aguirre, Francis Blanco, Philip of Jesus of Mexico, Gonzalo García of India, and you holy seventeen Japanese members of the Third Order, Saints Anthony of Nagasaki, Bonaventure, Cosmas, Francis of Fahelante, Francis of Miyako, Gabriel, Joachim, John, Leo, Louis, Matthias, Michael, Paul Ibaraki, Paul Zuzuki, Peter, Thomas Danki, and Thomas Kosaki, Protomartyrs of Japan, (1597 - Feb. 6)
*pray for us!*

Saints John Jones and John Wall, Martyrs of England, (1598 and 1679 - July 12)
*pray for us!*

Saint Fidelis of Sigmaringen, Protomartyr of the Sacred Congregation of the Propagation of the Faith, (1622 - April 24)
*pray for us!*

Saint Maximilian Kolbe, Martyr of Auschwitz (1941-August 14)
*pray for us!*

All you holy priests of the First Franciscan Order,
*pray for us!*

Saint Anthony of Padua, Doctor of the Gospel and Wonderworker, (1231 - June 13)
*pray for us!*

Saint Bonaventure, Seraphic Doctor, (1274 - July 15)
*pray for us!*

Saint Benvenute of Osimo, Bishop, (1282 - March 22)
*pray for us!*

Saint Louis of Tolouse, Bishop, (1297 - Aug. 19)
*pray for us!*

Saint Bernardine of Siena, (1444 - May 20)
*pray for us!*

Saint John Capistran, (1456 - Oct. 23)
*pray for us!*

Saint Peter Regalado, (1456 - March 30)
*pray for us!*

Saint James of the March, (1476 - Nov. 28)
*pray for us!*

Saint Peter of Alcantara, (1562 - Oct. 19)
*pray for us!*

Saint Francis Solano, (1610 - July 14)
*pray for us!*

Saint Joseph of Leonissa, (1612 - Feb. 4)
*pray for us!*

Saint Lawrence of Brindisi, Doctor of the Church, (1619 - July 21)
*pray for us!*

Saint Joseph of Cupertino, (1663 - Sept. 18)
*pray for us!*

Saint Pacificus of San Severino, (1721 - Sept. 24)
*pray for us!*

Saint John Joseph of the Cross, (1734 - March 5)
*pray for us!*

Saint Theophilus of Corte, (1740 - May 19)
*pray for us!*

Saint Leonard of Port Maurice, (1751 - Nov. 26)
*pray for us!*

Saint Leopold Mandic, (1942-May 12)
*pray for us!*

All you holy lay brothers of the First Franciscan Order,
*pray for us!*

Saint Didacus of Alcalá, (1463 - Nov. 7)
*pray for us!*

Saint Salvator of Horta, (1567 - March 18)
*pray for us!*

Saint Felix of Cantalice, (1585 - May 18)
*pray for us!*

Saint Benedict the Black, (1589 - April 3)
*pray for us!*

Saint Paschal Baylon, (1592 - May 17)
*pray for us!*

Saint Seraphin of Montegranaro, (1604 - Oct. 12)
*pray for us!*

Saint Charles of Sezze, (1670 - Jan. 6)
*pray for us!*

*Saint Ignatius Laconi, (1781 - May 11)*
*pray for us!*

Saint Francis Camporosso, (1866 - Sept. 20)
*pray for us!*

Saint Conrad of Parzham, (1894 - April 21)
*pray for us!*

\* \* \*

All you holy virgins of the Second Franciscan Order,
*pray for us!*

Holy Mother Clare of Assisi, (1253 - Aug. 11)
*pray for us!*

Saint Agnes of Assisi, (1253 - Nov. 19)
*pray for us!*

Saint Colette of Corbie, (1447 - Feb. 7)
*pray for us!*

Saint Catherine of Bologna, (1463 - May 9)
*pray for us!*

Saint Veronica Giuliani, (1727 - July 10)
*pray for us!*

\*　　\*　　\*

All you holy priests of the Third Franciscan Order,
  *pray for us!*
Saint Yves of Brittany, (1303 - May 19)
  *pray for us!*
Saint Charles Borromeo, Archbishop and Cardinal, (1584 - Nov. 4)
  *pray for us!*
Saint Joseph Benedict Cottolengo, (1842 - April 30)
  *pray for us!*
Saint Vincent Palotti, Founder, (1850 - Jan. 22)
  *pray for us!*
Saint John Mary Vianney, Patron of Parish Priests, (1859 - Aug. 4)
  *pray for us!*
Saint Joseph Cafasso, (1860 - June 23)
  *pray for us!*
Saint Michael Garicoits, (1863 - May 14)
  *pray for us!*
Saint Peter Julian Eymard, Founder, (1868 - Aug. 3)
  *pray for us!*
Saint John Bosco, Founder, (1883 - Jan. 31)
  *pray for us!*

Saint Pius X, Pope, (1914 - Aug. 21)
*pray for us!*

All you holy foundresses of religious congregations who were members of the Third Franciscan Order,
*pray for us!*

Saint Bridget of Sweden, (1373 - July 23)
*pray for us!*

Saint Jane of Valois, (1505 - Feb. 14)
*pray for us!*

Saint Angela Merici, (1540 - Jan. 27)
*pray for us!*

Saint Mary Bartholomea Capitanio, (1833 - July 26)
*pray for us!*

Saint Mary Magdalen Postel, (1846 - July 16)
*pray for us!*

Saint Vincentia Gerosa, (1847 - June 28)
*pray for us!*

Saint Joachima de Mas y de Vedruna, (1854 - May 22)
*pray for us!*

Saint Mary Josepha Rossello, (1880 - Oct. 3)
*pray for us!*

Saint Frances Xavier Cabrini, (1917 - Nov. 13)
*pray for us!*

\*　　　\*　　　\*

All you holy men of the Third Franciscan Order,
*pray for us!*

Saint Ferdinand, King of Castile and Leon, (1252 - May 30)
*pray for us!*

Saint Louis, King of France, Patron of the Third Order, (1270 - Aug. 25)
*pray for us!*

Saint Elzear of Sabran, (1323 - Sept. 26)
*pray for us!*

Saint Roch of Montpellier, (1327 - Aug. 16)
*pray for us!*

Saint Conrad of Piacenza, Hermit, (1351 - Feb. 19)
*pray for us!*

\*　　\*　　\*

All you holy women of the Third Franciscan Order,
*pray for us!*

Saint Elizabeth of Hungary, Patroness of the Third Order, (1231 - Nov. 19)
*pray for us!*

Saint Rose of Viterbo, Virgin, (1252 - Sept. 4)
*pray for us!*

Saint Zita of Lucca, Virgin, (1278 - April 27)
*pray for us!*

Saint Margaret of Cortona, (1297 - May 16)
  *pray for us!*
Saint Clare of Montefalco, Virgin and Religious, (1308 - Aug. 17)
  *pray for us!*
Saint Elizabeth of Portugal, (1336 - July 4)
  *pray for us!*
Saint Joan of Arc, Virgin, (1431 - May 30)
  *pray for us!*
Saint Frances of Rome, (1440 - March 9)
  *pray for us!*
Saint Catherine of Genoa, (1510 - Sept. 15)
  *pray for us!*
Saint Hyacintha Mariscotti, Virgin and Religious, (1640 - Jan. 30)
  *pray for us!*
Saint Mariana of Jesus of Quito, Virgin, (1645 - May 28)
  *pray for us!*
Saint Mary Frances of the Five Wounds, Virgin, (1791 - Oct. 6)
  *pray for us!*

\*     \*     \*

All you holy Cordbearers of St. Francis,
  *pray for us!*
Saint Frances de Sales, Bishop, (1622 - Jan. 24)
  *pray for us!*

Saint Joseph Calasanctius, Founder, (1648 - Aug. 25)
*pray for us!*
Saint Benedict Joseph Labre, (1783 - April 17)
*pray for us!*
Saint Bernadette Soubirous, Virgin and Religious, (1879 - April 16)
*pray for us!*

\*　　\*　　\*

Lamb of God, you take away the sins of the world,
*have mercy on us!*
Lamb of God, you take away the sins of the world,
*have mercy on us!*
Lamb of God, you take away the sins of the world,
*grant us peace!*

### Let us pray:

Almighty everlasting God, we thank you for granting us the joy of honoring our holy Father Francis and his sainted followers and enjoying the protection of their unceasing prayers. Grant us also the grace to imitate their example and so attain their fellowship in eternal glory. We ask this through Christ our Lord. Amen.

## LITANY OF ST. FRANCIS
### (for private devotion)

Lord have mercy on us!
  *Christ, have mercy on us!*
Lord, have mercy on us!
Christ, hear us!
  *Christ, graciously hear us!*
God, the Father of Heaven,
  *Have mercy on us!*
God, the Son, Redeemer of the world,
  *Have mercy on us!*
God, the Holy Spirit,
  *Have mercy on us!*
Holy Trinity, one God,
  *Have mercy on us!*
Holy Mary, conceived without sin,*
Holy Mary, special patron of the three Orders
  of St. Francis,
St. Francis, seraphic founder,
St. Francis, most prudent father,
St. Francis, who despised the world,
St. Francis, model of penance,
St. Francis, conqueror of vices,
  *Pray for us!*
St. Francis, imitator of our Savior,
St. Francis, bearer of the marks of Christ,

St. Francis, sealed with the character of Jesus.
St. Francis, example of purity,
St. Francis, image of humility,
St. Francis, abounding in grace,
St. Francis, who cured the sick,
St. Francis, who reformed the erring,
St. Francis, pillar of the Church,
St. Francis, who defended the Faith,
St. Francis, champion of Christ,
St. Francis, protector of your children,
St. Francis, invulnerable shield,
St. Francis, who confounded the heretics,
St. Francis, who converted the pagans,
St. Francis, who supported the lame,
St. Francis, who raised the dead,
St. Francis, who healed the lepers,
St. Francis, our advocate,

Lamb of God, who take away the sins of the world, *Spare us, O Lord!*

Lamb of God, who take away the sins of the world, *Graciously hear us, O Lord!*

Lamb of God, who take away the sins of the world, *Have mercy on us!*

**V.** Pray for us, blessed Father Francis.

**R.** That we may be made worthy of the promises of Christ.

Let us pray:

O Lord Jesus Christ, who, when the world was growing cold, in order to inflame our hearts with the fire of your love, renewed the sacred marks of your suffering on the body of our blessed father Francis, mercifully grant that by his merits and prayers we may persevere in bearing the cross, and bring forth worthy fruits of penance. Who live and reign world without end. Amen.

## LITANY OF ST. ANTHONY
### (for private devotion)

Lord, have mercy on us!
*Christ, have mercy on us!*
Lord, have mercy on us!
Christ, hear us!
*Christ, graciously hear us!*
God, the Father of Heaven,
*Have mercy on us!*
God, the Son, Redeemer of the world,
*Have mercy on us!*
God, the Holy Spirit,
*Have mercy on us!*
Holy Trinity, one God,
*Have mercy on us!*

Holy Mary, conceived without sin,*
St. Anthony of Padua,
St. Anthony, glory of the Franciscan Order,
St. Anthony, lily of virginity,
St. Anthony, gem of poverty,
St. Anthony, example of obedience,
St. Anthony, mirror of abstinence,
St. Anthony, vessel of purity,
St. Anthony, star of sanctity,
St. Anthony, model of perfection,
St. Anthony, ark of the Testament,
St. Anthony, keeper of the Scriptures,
St. Anthony, teacher of truth,
St. Anthony, preacher of grace,
St. Anthony, exterminator of vices,
St. Anthony, planter of virtues,
St. Anthony, hammer of heretics,
St. Anthony, deliverer of captives,
St. Anthony, guide of the erring,
St. Anthony, comforter of the afflicted,
St. Anthony, healer of the sick,
St. Anthony, counselor of the erring,
St. Anthony, searcher of consciences,
St. Anthony, martyr in desire,
St. Anthony, terror of demons,
St. Anthony, horror of Hell,

---

*Pray for us!*

St. Anthony, performer of miracles,

St. Anthony, restorer of lost things,

St. Anthony, helper of all who invoke you,

Lamb of God, who take away the sins of the world, *Spare us, O Lord!*

Lamb of God, who take away the sins of the world, *Graciously hear us, O Lord!*

Lamb of God, who take away the sins of the world, *Have mercy on us!*

**V.** Pray for us, blessed Anthony,

**R.** That we may be made worthy of the promises of Christ.

Let us pray:

Almighty and eternal God, who have glorified your faithful confessor and doctor Anthony with the perpetual gift of working miracles, graciously grant that what we confidently seek through his merits, we may surely receive upon his intercession. Through Christ our Lord. Amen.

(Other prayers to St. Anthony are on pages 234-236).

# CALENDAR OF
# FRANCISCAN SAINTS

# CALENDAR OF FRANCISCAN SAINTS

Abbreviations used are the following: OFM for Order of Friars Minor (Franciscans); Conv for Conventual Franciscans; Cap for Capuchin Franciscans; TOR for Third Order Regular; I Ord for First Franciscan Order; II Ord for Second Franciscan Order (Poor Clares and other branches of the Second Order); III Ord for the Third Order Secular of St. Francis.

Franciscan saints honored in the Roman calendar are indicated by Rom.

An obligatory memorial is indicated simply by Memorial; and when the memorial is optional, the abbreviation Opt Memorial is used.

## JANUARY

1. Solemnity of the Mother of God.
3. Holy Name of Jesus. Memorial

7. Bl Angela of Foligno, religious of III Ord (Opt Memorial for III Ord)
12. Bl Bernard of Corleone, religious of I Ord. Opt Memorial
14. Bl Odoric of Pordenone, priest of I Ord. Opt Memorial
16. Sts Berard, priest, and companions, proto-martyrs of I Ord. Memorial
24. St Francis de Sales, bishop, doctor, Cord-bearer of St. Francis. Memorial (Rom)
27. St Angela Merici, virgin of III Ord, founder. Memorial (Rom)
30. St Hyacinth of Mariscotti, virgin of III Ord (Opt Memorial for III Ord).
31. St John Bosco, priest of III Ord, founder. Memorial (Rom)

## FEBRUARY

4. St Joseph of Leonissa, priest of I Ord. Opt Memorial
6. Sts Peter Baptist, Paul Miki, and companions, martyrs of I and III Ord. Memorial
7. St Colette, virgin of II Ord (Feast for Colettines; Memorial for II and III Ord Nuns).
19. St. Conrad of Piacenza, hermit of III Ord (Opt Memorial for III Ord)

# MARCH

2. Bl Agnes of Prague, virgin of II Ord (Opt Memorial for II and III Ord nuns)
9. St Frances of Rome, religious of III Ord. Opt Memorial (Rom)
24. Bl Didacus Joseph of Cadiz, priest of I Ord. Opt Memorial

# APRIL

3. St Benedict the Black, religious of 1 Ord. Memorial
16. St Bernadette Soubirous, Cordbearer of St. Francis.
17. St Benedict Joseph Labre, Cordbearer of St Francis.
21. St Conrad of Parzham, religious of I Ord. Memorial
23. Bl Giles of Assisi, religious of I Ord. Opt Memorial
24. St Fidelis of Sigmaringen, priest and martyr of I Ord. Feast
28. Bl Luchesius, layman of III Ord (Opt Memorial for the III Ord).

# MAY

9. St Catherine of Bologna, virgin of III Ord (Memorial for II and III Ord nuns).
11. St Ignatius of Laconi, religious of I Ord. Opt Memorial

16. St Margaret of Cortona, member of III Ord. Memorial.
17. St Paschal Baylon, religious of I Ord. Memorial
18. St Felix of Cantalice, religious of I Ord. Feast.
20. St Bernadine of Siena, priest of I Ord. Feast
24. Dedication of Basilica of St. Francis of Assisi. Feast
28. St Mariana of Jesus de Paredes, virgin of III Ord. Opt Memorial
30. Bl Baptista Varano, virgin of II Ord (Opt Memorial for II and III Ord nuns)
30. St Ferdinand, king, member of III Ord

## JUNE

12. Bl Jolenta, religious of II Ord (Opt Memorial for II and III Order nuns)
13. St Anthony of Padua, priest and doctor of I Ord. Feast.
22. St Thomas More, martyr of the III Ord, with St John Fisher. Opt Memorial (Rom)
30. Bl Raymond Lull, martyr of III Ord (Opt Memorial for III Ord)

## JULY

8. Bl Gregory Grassi, bishop, and com-

panions, martyrs of I and III Ord. Opt Memorial

9. St Nicholas Pick, priest, and companions, martyrs of I Ord. Memorial

10. St Veronica Giuliani, virgin of II Ord. Memorial (Feast for II and III Ord nuns)

12. Sts John Jones and John Wall, priests and martyrs of I Ord. Opt Memorial

13. Bl Angeline of Marsciano, religious of III Ord. Memorial for III Ord nuns.

14. St Francis Solano, priest of I Ord. Opt Memorial

15. St Bonaventure, bishop and doctor of I Ord. Feast.

21. St Lawrence of Brindisi, priest and doctor of I Ord. Feast.

23. Bl Cunegunda, religious of II Ord. Opt Memorial for II and III Ord nuns

23. St Bridget, widow of III Ord, founder. Opt Memorial (Rom)

24. Bl Louise of Savoy, religious of II Ord. Opt Memorial for II and III Ord nuns

27. Bl Mary Magdalene of Martinegro, virgin of II Ord. Opt Memorial for II and III Ord nuns

# AUGUST

2. Our Lady of the Angels of Portiuncula. Feast.
4. St John Baptist Mary Vianney, priest of III Ord. Memorial (Rom)
7. Bls Agathangelus and Cassian, priests and martyrs of I Ord. Opt Memorial
8. Holy Father Dominic, priest founder of the Order of Preachers, Feast
11. St Clare of Assisi, virgin of II Ord. Feast (Solemnity for II and III Ord nuns).
14. St Maximilian Kolbe, priest of I Ord. Memorial
17. St Roch, member of III Ord
19. St Louis, bishop of I Ord. Memorial
21. St Pius X, pope, member of III Ord. Memorial (Rom)
25. St Louis IX, king, member and patron of III Ord. Memorial.

# SEPTEMBER

1. Bl Beatrice of Silva, virgin of II Ord, founder. Opt Memorial
2. Bls John Francis Burte, Severin Girault, and companions, martyrs of I and III Ord. Opt Memorial

4. St Rose of Viterbo, virgin of III Ord. Opt Memorial for III Ord.
17. Stigmata of our holy Father Francis. Feast.
18. St Joseph of Cupertino, priest of I Ord. Feast.
20. St Francis Mary of Camporosso, religious of I Ord. Memorial
23. Finding of Body of St. Clare. Opt Memorial for II and III Ord Nuns
26. St Elzear of Sabran and Bl Delphine, husband and wife of III Ord. Opt Memorial for III Ord

## OCTOBER

4. Our Holy Father Francis, deacon, founder of Three Franciscan Orders. Solemnity.
6. St Mary Frances of the Five Wounds, virgin of III Ord. Opt Memorial for III Ord
10. Sts Daniel, priest, and companions, martyrs of I Ord. Opt Memorial
12. St Seraphin of Montegranaro, religious of I Ord. Opt Memorial
20. Bl James of Strepar, bishop of I Ord. Opt Memorial
20. Bl Contardo Ferrini, member of III Ord. Opt Memorial for III Ord
21. Bl Josephine Leroux, virgin and martyr of

II Ord. Opt Memorial for II and III Ord Nuns

22. St Peter of Alcantara, priest of I Ord. Memorial

23. St John of Capistrano, priest of I Ord. Memorial

26. Bl Bonaventure of Potenza, priest of I Ord. Opt Memorial

30. Anniversary of Dedication in Consecrated Franciscan Churches. Solemnity

## NOVEMBER

4. St Charles Borromeo, bishop of III Ord. Memorial (Rom)

7. St Didacus of Alcala, religious of I Ord. Opt Memorial

13. St Frances Xavier Cabrini, virgin of III Ord. founder. Memorial in the U.S. (Rom)

14. Sts Nicholas Tavelic, priest, and companions, martyrs of I Ord. Memorial

17. St Elizabeth of Hungary, widow, member and patron of III Ord. Feast.

18. Bl Salome, virgin of II Ord. Opt Memorial for II Ord and III Ord nuns

19. St Agnes of Assisi, virgin of II Ord. Opt Memorial (Memorial for II and III Ord nuns).

24. Commemoration of all the Deceased of the Franciscan Orders. Memorial
26. St Leonard of Port Maurice, priest of I Order. Memorial
27. St Francis Anthony Fasani, priest of I Ord. Opt Memorial
28. St James of the March, priest of I Ord. Memorial
29. All Saints of the Franciscan Orders. Feast.

## DECEMBER

8. Immaculate Conception of the Blessed Virgin Mary, Patron and Queen of the Franciscan Orders. Solemnity (Rom)
12. Our Lady of Guadalupe, Patron and Queen of the Americas. Memorial in the U.S. (Rom)
15. Bl Mary Frances Schervier, virgin of III Ord. Opt Memorial for III Ord

**NOTE:** Feasts and memorials of saints and blessed are not celebrated when they are superseded by a Sunday or a feast of higher rank. During the first five and a half weeks of Lent and from Dec. 17 to 31, memorials of saints and blessed are not celebrated in the divine office and holy Mass, but may be commemorated at Lauds and their oration may be substituted for the oration of the day at

Mass. During Holy Week and Easter Week, feasts and memorials of saints and blessed are entirely omitted in that year, except a titular feast which is transferred to the first open day.

**NOTES**

**NOTES**

**NOTES**

**NOTES**

# NOTES

**NOTES**

**NOTES**

**NOTES**

**NOTES**

# NOTES

**NOTES**

# NOTES